Praise for *CFA® Confidential*

"Entertaining and instructive. . ."

> **—Charles Brandes, CFA**
> Chairman
> Brandes Investment Partners, L.P.

"The CFA ethics education reinforced my foundation to make more difficult stock calls. I strongly recommend the CFA charter and hope *CFA Confidential* will help to advertise its many benefits."

> **—Mike Mayo, CFA**
> Bank Analyst & 2013 CFA Award Winner for Ethics and Standards of Investment Practice
> CLSA

"Greg's cost/benefit analysis of the CFA designation versus an MBA is worth the price of admission. This book is an honest introspection on the process of obtaining a CFA charter. Its authenticity is so accurate, my stomach knotted when reading about the exam day details. An entertaining and informative read."

> **—Jeffrey deGraaf, CMT, CFA**
> Chairman/CEO
> Renaissance Macro Research, LLC

"Greg's wealth of experience—both good and not so good—within the CFA program has led to a highly entertaining handbook that every CFA candidate should read before taking a single step on their own journey."

> **—Bill Thompson, CFA**
> President and Portfolio Manager
> Round Table Investment Management Company

"Anyone thinking about trying for their CFA Charter will enjoy reading about the highs and lows of Greg's journey and the insight it provides into the overall process. Becoming a CFA Charterholder is one of the most difficult tasks one will face in life, and Greg does a great job at providing an insider's view."

—**Daniel A. Ward, CFA**
Director of Investments
Virginia Tech Foundation

"Although I went through the ordeal of getting a CFA back in the '90s, I wish I'd read this book before I embarked on the campaign. The practical advice on how to work effectively throughout the arduous process is extremely helpful and could be the most important factor for many candidates between passing the tests and getting through all three levels of the exam—or not. It might seem irrelevant initially, but having the proper chair, creating a calm work space, setting up a study timeline, and dealing with the psychological pitfalls are just the sorts of things which are critical to success in the pursuit of the designation."

—**Anthony Leggett, CFA**
International Equity PM
Oechsle International Advisors

"The question of whether to pursue the CFA and its benefits compared to grad school is a common one for many professionals starting their careers. *CFA Confidential* does a nice job laying out the pros and cons and is a helpful tool to those dealing with this important question."

—**Daniel Farley, CFA**
Senior Managing Director
Chief Investment Officer—Investment Solutions Group
Boston-based investment firm

"*CFA Confidential* is an entertaining and insightful guide that explains the ins and outs of the CFA Program. An absolute must-read for every CFA candidate."

—**Chris Lafemina, CFA**

CFA® Confidential: What It *Really* Takes to Become a Chartered Financial Analyst®

Gregory M. Campion, CFA

For Whitney, who put up with me studying for five years and then writing this book. Thank you and I'm sorry!

Table of Contents

About the Author

A CFA Charterholder®, Greg Campion honed his investment skills on the trading floors of Lehman Brothers, becoming a trusted capital markets advisor to some of the savviest hedge fund and mutual fund investors in the business. His investment commentary has been widely read by many of Wall Street's most influential investors. Campion is a graduate of Stonehill College and earned an MBA in Finance from New York University's Stern School of Business. He currently lives in Charlotte, North Carolina, with his family.

Preface

I wrote this book to help people. Having spent five years of my life pursuing and ultimately attaining the CFA Charter®, I learned a few things—a few things besides the intricacies of pricing swaps, that is. It's no understatement to refer to the process of attaining your charter as utterly exhausting, frustrating, disappointing, gut-wrenching, boring, and lonely. But the process can also be incredibly rewarding, uplifting, character defining, and enlightening.

I won't sugarcoat it. Studying for the CFA® is brutal. I know because I suffered through it six painful times. But I think that what I've learned along the way can help you. Whether you are contemplating entering the CFA Program®, are knee-deep in the process, or know someone who is, the insights in this book can help you.

If you are embarking on the road to your charter, I can't promise that these tips will guarantee that you'll pass these tests. All the advice in the world can't stand in for the hard work and dedication you'll need to invest in this process. But I'm confident that my insights might just help you avoid some of the stupid mistakes that I made, stay (somewhat) sane, and maybe even figure out how to laugh about this ridiculous undertaking that you are subjecting yourself to.

I hope that the thoughts I share in the following pages will provide you with a voice of reason, guidance, and commiseration. I also encourage you to share this book with your family, spouse, and significant others. As you may already know, attaining the CFA charter is in many ways a one-man (or one-woman) show, but in many other ways it absolutely is not possible without the support of the people who love you. I wish you the best of luck.

Prologue

As I sat in a dimly lit hotel ballroom in Boston's Back Bay district, I felt like I was losing control of my own thoughts. Crowded in among hundreds of other poor souls who were collectively experiencing one of the most nerve-racking days of their lives, I tried to get my bearings. The afternoon session of the exam would begin in ten minutes. The mood was tense. Chitchat was minimal. The man to my left sat so still with his eyes closed that if it weren't for the occasional deep breath, I could have sworn he had expired right then and there, a victim of CFA stress. The woman to my right was also void of any outward emotion—she sat stiffly with a military-like posture staring straight ahead. Her perfectly aligned pens, pencils, erasers, and calculator gave the impression that she'd done this a thousand times before—and intimidated the hell out me.

It was 2011 and I had been on the hunt for my CFA charter for four long years. This was exam day, the culmination of all my hard work and sacrifice. It was the third and final level. The morning session had been rough, but I knew that the material on the afternoon session was my strength and I expected to do well. Failure was not an option. I'd already failed this level once. If I failed this time around, I figured, it wasn't meant to be. How embarrassing it would be to fail it again. I sure as hell couldn't stomach another six months of studying. I couldn't fail. I wouldn't fail.

The minutes ticked by ever so slowly. The instructions were read over the loudspeaker. Bubble in your name and your candidate number. Rip out the answer sheet along the perforated line. Everything was going according to plan when a careless mistake sent me into a panicked spiral—I had just torn out an extra page of my answer booklet. I panicked. I looked around for help. "This is not a big deal," I tried to convince myself. But it was. A proctor arrived at my desk and took my exam book. "We'll get you another one," she said.

And then the exam started. But I had no book. One minute. Two minutes. Three minutes. Nothing. Finally, five minutes into the exam, my test book arrived.

But it was too late. Panic had taken over. I tried to read the opening passages of the Ethics material, but I just couldn't concentrate. I was breathing fast, and my heart was beating out of control. This Ethics section suddenly seemed impossible.

Ethics was normally a part of the exam that I considered a strength, and I counted on a strong performance here so I could "bank" extra minutes to use later. But I was so flustered at this point that I could hardly read the questions. What I did read seemed to make no sense at all. To top it off, the stress was taking over and I was experiencing severe chest pains. A perfectly healthy thirty-three-year-old man should not be experiencing chest pains. Was I having a heart attack? At least, I thought grimly, dropping dead on the spot would save me from the shame of failing once again.

CHAPTER 1:

CFA® Dreams

* Back Where It All Began
* What is the CFA Charter?
* What's on the Test?
* Pass Rates
* Three Hundred Hours
* And WHY Would I Do This?
* Those Magical Three Letters
* "A Terrible Idea"
* R-E-S-P-E-C-T

BACK WHERE IT ALL BEGAN

How did I get in this mess? Let's wind the clock back to early 2007. I was working for Lehman Brothers in New York City, trying to figure out what to do with the rest of my life. I had been lucky enough to backdoor my way into the securities industry seven years earlier after having graduated from a small liberal arts school in Massachusetts. I'd been living in the center of the universe that is New York City since 2001 and had it pretty good. I was in international equity sales, which basically meant that I got to spend my days talking about stocks and interacting with some of the smartest investors on the planet. I worked in one of those hubs of human activity they call a trading floor, and for a young guy in his twenties, I was even making halfway decent money.

My nights were spent in the classroom. I was pursuing an MBA at NYU Stern and was due to finish up in the fall of 2007. I had also been lucky enough to strike gold in my personal life. A year earlier, I had been set up with the girl of my dreams, Whitney. Whitney was from South Carolina but had been in NYC for five years herself. She was also in the investment banking world, and worked at a rival firm.

For some ungodly reason, it was around this time I got the idea in my head that I should enroll in the CFA Program. What was I thinking?

WHAT IS THE CFA CHARTER?

If you haven't ever studied for a CFA exam or known someone who has, you might be wondering what all the fuss is about. Why are people so infatuated with this test? What do they get if they pass? And is it really *that* hard?

These are all legitimate questions and I'll do my best to answer them. First of all, the CFA Program, which is what candidates must battle their way through to become charterholders, traces its roots back to 1963, when 268 trailblazing candidates passed the first CFA exam.[1]

Since then, the CFA Program has seen rapid growth. In 2012 alone, there were over 200,000 people worldwide who registered for various levels of the CFA. That is a small number compared

---

[1]Source: Nancy Regan, *The Gold Standard: A Fifty-Year History of the CFA Charter* (China: BW&A Books, Inc., 2012).

to the hoards of people who pursue designations and degrees like the CPA, MBA, and others, but to put it in context, there are fewer than 120,000 charterholders worldwide. So the number of people who registered for CFA exams in 2012 equates to almost double the number of existing CFA charterholders—and as I said, people have been taking these exams since 1963!

To attain that title of charterholder, these folks had to jump through some serious hoops. The CFA Program consists of three separate six-hour examinations. The Level 1 exam is offered every June and every December. Levels 2 and 3 are offered only once per year, in June.

WHAT'S ON THE TEST?

The material that candidates need to master to earn their charter is almost unbelievably broad in scope yet also incredibly detailed in terms of how well candidates need to know each concept.

The material for each exam is covered in the "curriculum" for that given level. The curriculum is a set of very thick books (typically five or six of them) filled with just about every investment- or finance-related concept known to man. There is a separate curriculum to master for each of the three levels.

Concepts range from things that you might expect, like Economics, Accounting, Statistics, and Corporate Finance, to subjects that might surprise you, like the intricacies of Pension Accounting (and there are plenty of intricacies!), the most tax-efficient ways to transfer wealth between generations, Behavioral Finance, and Ethics.

A quick perusal of the curriculum, with its hundreds of mind-blowing formulas that must be committed to memory, leaves most people intimidated if not flat-out dumbfounded. It doesn't seem possible that any one human being could commit so much complex material to memory, yet thousands of candidates do exactly that year in and year out.

In addition to the curriculum, most candidates use other resources to help them increase their chances of passing. Third-party study notes are one of the most common tools. These are effectively set up in a similar fashion to the curriculum (i.e., five or six books, covering the material in roughly the same order), but they attempt to do it in a much more succinct and digestible manner. Many candidates exclusively use these third-party notes to study from.

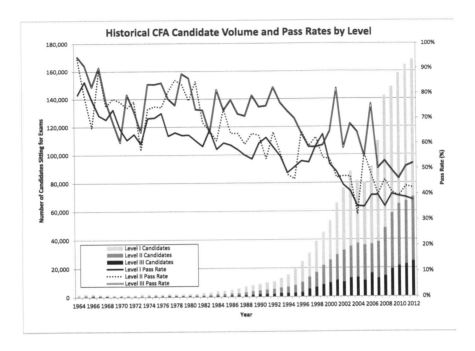

PASS RATES

No matter which method they choose, **most of these candidates will fail.** Only about a fifth of the candidates who sign up for Level 1 will *ever* earn their charter. In fact, only 38% of candidates passed Level 1 in 2012. Levels 2 and 3 weren't much better with pass rates of only 42% and 52%, respectively. Statistically speaking, if you began taking CFA exams in 2010, your chance of passing all three in a row was less than 9%.[2]

The discouraging thing for many candidates is that while Level 1 may be a weeding-out stage, the Level 2 and 3 pass rates are also depressingly low when considering that candidates are up against a group of people who have *already* passed Level 1 (no small task itself), as opposed to the general population. In other words, the

---

[2]Assumes an average pass rate of 39% for Level 1 in 2010 (actual pass rates for the exam, which is offered twice annually, were 2010A: 42%; 2010B: 36%); as well as the actual pass rates for Level 2 in 2011 (43%) and Level 3 in 2012 (52%). See index for historical pass rate data.

weeding-out has already happened, yet the pass rates for Levels 2 and 3 remain shockingly low.

The chart on page 4 shows you historical pass rates by level as well as the number of candidates sitting for each exam. The declining pass rates are likely the result of many factors including a mass influx of Level 1 candidates, many of whom are not prepared for the trials and tribulations of the CFA Program. The internationalization of the CFA Program is also likely to be a factor as more candidates are taking the exams in a language other than their primary one.

THREE HUNDRED HOURS

And then of course there is the issue of how much time it takes to prepare for each exam. The conventional wisdom is that 250-300 hours of study time are needed per level. For most candidates, that basically means ALL of their free time for the six months leading up to exam day. Simply put, this test dominates the lives of the people who choose to take it on.

I was no exception. The CFA Program dominated my life. And sadly, I was not among the lucky few who make it through without failing an exam. I was fortunate enough to pass Level 1 my first time through, but that would be the only level I emerged from unscathed. Level 2 took me two attempts, which is fairly normal. But Level 3 was where my mettle was really tested. It took me *three long years* and *three grueling attempts* to get past that final level. The process, as I'll explain later, took absolutely every ounce of determination, stamina, and grit that I could possibly muster.

AND WHY WOULD I DO THIS?

So WHY on earth do so many people subject themselves to this torturous process every year? Simply put, it's because the CFA charter has become the "gold standard" of the investment world. Candidates interested in pursuing or furthering careers in investment banking, portfolio management, investment consulting, or any number of related fields will find themselves with a distinct advantage over the competition upon earning their charters. The CFA charter is recognized, respected, and many times required by some of the most prestigious financial firms on the planet and is only growing in popularity. Rightly or wrongly, many candidates see the CFA Program as a fast track to success and wealth.

Later in the book, I'll talk about whether or not I think the sacrifices that candidates make to become charterholders are worth it. I'll discuss what I think are the most important things I took away from my experience in the CFA Program (hint: it's not the investment knowledge). And I'll try to guide you through some common-sense methods that might help you to come up with a plan to conquer this seemingly impossible task if you decide to take it on.

But for now, all you need to know about the CFA Program is that . . . well . . . it's kind of a big deal.

THOSE MAGICAL THREE LETTERS

Signing up for the CFA Program was something I'd thought about over the years, but it always seemed so unattainable. In fact, three or four years before I ever sat for the Level 1 exam, I had signed up for a CFA class, but when I showed up on the first night of class I was blown away. Everyone there appeared to be a hundred times smarter than me, and it seemed like the instructor was speaking a foreign language. It was like being in one of those really bad dreams from which you wake up in a cold sweat. I never went back.

That didn't stop me from being endlessly impressed by the buy-side portfolio managers and analysts I met with regularly who sported the "CFA" after their names. The sell-side analysts I worked with had the same three letters adorning their business cards, and I felt somehow inferior without such impressive credentials.

In equity sales, you sometimes feel less than useful because you attend meetings with some seriously smart people, but you don't always get to say that much. Sometimes you'll arrange a meeting for a sell-side analyst and a buy-side analyst, and then you'll sit in the room with the two of them and try not to cough. The problem is not that you're clueless, you're just not an expert in *every* sector. For instance, I'd take my telecoms analyst, who spent every day thinking about telecoms, to meet with a buy-side analyst at a large mutual fund company who covered telecoms and therefore spent *his* day, every day, thinking about telecoms. Because I wasn't a telecoms expert, there was only so much I'd be able to add to the discussion, and this could be frustrating.

I did, however, learn an incredible amount by attending hundreds of these meetings every year. I learned about every industry, from banking to telecoms to natural resources, and I learned how really smart people think and present ideas to one another. But still, I envied the CFA designation on my colleagues' business cards, and perhaps I felt a bit inadequate for not being an expert on each and every sector. The CFA charter, in my mind at least, had a magical quality. Perhaps the difficulty of obtaining it was part of what ultimately drove me to pursue it.

"A TERRIBLE IDEA"

Around this time, Whitney and I were discussing leaving New York. She was keen on a move to North Carolina, having grown up in the South. But moving to the South was such an extreme thought for me, having grown up in Connecticut, that I couldn't really fathom it at the time. We had also started looking at the possibility of other cities like Boston,[3] where I had spent a year after college, a city that always had a special place in my heart, not least of which was explained by my affinity for the local baseball team, the Red Sox.

But it was during this time, while we were still in New York contemplating our future, that I started thinking seriously about how I wanted to develop my career. "How hard can the CFA be?" I thought. I could work for Lehman for another couple of years, study for the exam at night, and maybe my employer would even help with the cost of the program.

I emailed Whitney one day while at work: "So, I'm thinking about taking the CFA. What do you think?" Having just had front-row seats to my business school experience, she immediately wrote me back: "That's a terrible idea."

The process of battling my way through business school had already been an immense effort. Hours upon hours of class time, group work, etc. It was a serious undertaking. The CFA, Whitney had the foresight to see, would be just as much of a struggle.

---

[3] As it turns out, after much negotiation and some suspect analysis on my part showing Whitney that Boston wasn't really *that* much colder than New York, we would ultimately relocate to the city famous for its baked beans, clam chowder, and "gawd"-awful accents, where Whitney would freeze her behind off for the next four years.

She told me how she had seen incredibly smart people fail CFA exams time and time again. She knew that I absolutely wasn't a "math guy." Despite being in investment banking, I probably had one of the least "financy" jobs on Wall Street. She'd seen me struggle through the heavily quantitative classes in business school, like Statistics and Accounting. She knew the CFA would be an absolute battle for me. Her prediction was rational, compassionate, and right.

I, of course, being the eternal optimist and dreamer, saw only the results. I didn't see the hours and hours of backbreaking (sometimes literally as you'll read later) studying. I didn't see the toll that it would take on relationships with my friends and my family. I didn't anticipate feeling disappointment and failure like I had never known before in my entire life.

R-E-S-P-E-C-T

No, I was blinded. I was blinded by those three letters. I envisioned myself as Gregory Campion, CFA. Who knew what I would do with those three letters? Maybe I'd go off and be a hedge fund manager and live in Greenwich and drive a Porsche. Maybe I'd move to Boston or some other city and go run an international equities portfolio and tell young analysts how they needed to work harder if they wanted to get where I am.

Or maybe I'd just get some respect. Maybe I didn't want a Porsche or a soapbox to stand on to shout orders at young analysts. In fact, I'm quite sure I didn't. Maybe I just wanted to walk into that meeting with the buy-side analyst and sell-side analyst, slap my business card, CFA credential and all, on the table, and instantaneously achieve an unspoken yet undeniable level of respect.

Kind of funny how a quest for a little bit of respect can drive a person, isn't it?

The rest, as they say, is history. I signed up for Level 1 that same week.

I can't tell you though how many times during my CFA-studying years Whitney looked at me and said, "I told you this was a terrible idea." To this, I ultimately would say, "Yep, you were right." But nonetheless, here I am a full-fledged CFA charterholder. It took me a few more attempts than I had planned. Three extra attempts to be precise, but I ultimately got it done. My intention, should you choose to take on this beast, is to help you do the same.

Chapter 1 Checklist:	
☑ **Do:**	☒ **Don't:**
☑ 1) Get the facts on the CFA Program before signing up. You need to understand what you're getting into.	☒ 1) Sign up first and ask questions later.
☑ 2) Think about the time commitment—300 hours per level—and whether or not you can fit this into your life.	☒ 2) Underestimate the time and effort attaining your charter really takes.
☑ 3) Consider that failing *at least* one test is not only possible, but likely.	☒ 3) Assume you'll glide through the CFA Program without any hiccups.

CHAPTER 2:

Knowing What You're Getting Into

* Just One Question: Why?

* Lying to Yourself

* What *Really* Motivates You?

* Working for a Living

* Not Enough Hours in the Day

* Getting Better at Your Job

* Life is Passing Me By

* Your Better Half

* The Offspring

* Your Mom Is Worried about You!

* Just a Friend

* A Little Effort Goes a Long Way

JUST ONE QUESTION: WHY?

If you've been thinking about getting your CFA charter, or you're in the process of studying for the exams, this is a good time to ask yourself one simple question: *Why?* Many people sign up for the exams, start studying, and may get years into the process before they ask themselves this simple question.

DO NOT simply gloss over this and worry about it later. Committing yourself to the CFA Program is absolutely not a decision to be taken lightly. This is not like deciding if you're going out for dinner tonight, or which movie you're going to see. Those decisions have consequences that usually last no more than twenty-four hours. The decision to embark upon the CFA journey is one that very well may have lifelong consequences, both positive and negative.

LYING TO YOURSELF

So what *is* your motivation for taking the CFA exams? If you're like me, you may be lying to yourself. When I first started talking about taking these tests, people would inevitably ask me "Why?" and I needed to come up with an answer.

Depending on the day or who I was talking to, that answer would change. To some people I'd say, "Well, you know I just finished up B-school, so this stuff is all fresh in my mind." In retrospect, that answer seems delusional. While there certainly is some overlapping material, the CFA is a beast unto itself. Having just earned an MBA may have some benefit, but that in itself is not a *reason* to take the CFA.

To others, I would say, "Well, I really want to bullet-proof my résumé." This had some element of truth to it. I like to think that back in 2007 I very wisely realized that the market was going to fall apart and jobs in finance would be much tougher to come by. Did I really predict that? Probably not, but I had been in the industry long enough to realize that it was a cyclical one. I had seen hordes of people laid off both in 2001 (post 9/11 and the dot-com boom) and then again in 2004. I was realistic that at some point, my number could be up.

I also saw the growing popularity of the CFA exam. Everyone on the sell-side has to have their Series 7, but as I saw so many young people starting to take the CFA, I thought, "Shoot, this thing might be required at some point. And I am sure as hell not studying for it when I'm forty."

Those are the reasons that I *like to think* drove me to take the CFA.

WHAT *REALLY* MOTIVATES YOU?

But were those the reasons that really drove me? Looking back now, I think the answer is no. I wanted respect. I wanted to feel competent. And I think, quite frankly, I was just awed by the CFA credential itself. It was so difficult to attain. It was so widely respected. And only the best and brightest were able to achieve it. In some strange way I was drawn to the CFA Program by the sheer difficulty of the process itself.

When it came to competence, I think I was somewhat paranoid about my own investment knowledge in the early part of my career. You see, I had pretty much landed on Wall Street without any formal finance training and was told *go*. Right out of Lehman's training program in 2001, I was covering hedge fund clients. I was responsible for calling portfolio managers who were often twenty or thirty years my senior and trying to advise them on markets. "How the hell can I tell these guys something they don't already know?" I wondered.

But I figured it out. I learned what type of information they needed, and I did my best to deliver it to them. I won't lie. There were many times when I found myself in conversations that were way over my head. This happened especially often during my first few years in the business when succeeding at my job really meant doing everything in my power not to be perceived as an incompetent idiot.

In order to become the expert I wanted to be, I felt that I really needed to supplement my knowledge base with a more formal education. I figured this would be the only way to get over this feeling of cluelessness that drove me insane.

So why do you need to know about my various insecurities and motivations? Because I'm willing to bet that you have some, too. Why are you taking this test? Think about it. REALLY think about it. Is it money? Is it respect? Or is it a quest for knowledge? Perhaps it's something completely different.

Heck, you might even be saying to yourself, "It's not the money. It's not the respect. It's not even the competence. It's just that my employer requires it!"

If that's the case, then you might even be in a more difficult situation. Whatever was ultimately responsible for my own insatiable drive to achieve the CFA designation did have one major advantage—it was inside of *me*. And, in my experience, the CFA Program is so trying, so all-consuming, that YOU need to want it. Not your employer. Not anybody else. You. So even if it's a required part of your job, I think a bit of soul-searching from an early stage is not a bad idea as *you* are ultimately in control of the path you take.

WORKING FOR A LIVING

So whether you're driven by money, or knowledge, or competence, or respect, most people take the CFA to better their career prospects. The problem, of course, is that the time commitment needed to pass the CFA exams will inevitably impact your performance at work. So ironically, while most people take the CFA to get a better job, their performance in their current job almost always suffers while they're studying. The key is balance.

My employer at the time wasn't really involved in the process. That is, they didn't finance it or even encourage it. They had paid for that initial CFA class years earlier as well as a large chunk of my business school tuition, but after some initial mulling over, I decided that the CFA was *my* thing. I would pay for it. I would study on my own time.

Of course, it's not that easy. As anyone who has taken any level of the CFA exam knows, these tests consume your life. They consume your personal life completely, and they consume your professional life quite a bit, too.

NOT ENOUGH HOURS IN THE DAY

Luckily I was able to continue to progress in my career while taking these exams. I had gotten pretty good at equity sales at this point, and for all intents and purposes, I could put things on autopilot when I needed to. I'm not saying that I was phoning it in, but I wasn't necessarily going above and beyond by putting in fifteen-hour days and working on weekends as I might have done before.

In my job, there was meant to be at least some entertaining of clients. Whether you were going to a baseball game or a show or just grabbing a drink, you were supposed to be out with clients a decent amount. While I was studying for the CFA exam—so basically six months out of the year for five years—I had to pare this way back. Of course, I still did lots of client coffees and lunches during the day, but my nights were mine. My weekends were mine. To be honest, I didn't feel like I was short-changing my employers during this process. Occasionally I'd have a really good outing with a client that led to valuable opportunities for the firm, but more often than not, it was time that, in all honesty, would probably have been better spent at home with my family.

The point of this is to tell you that I was no longer going above and beyond like I had prior to the CFA. There had been a time when I thought about my job constantly. On weekends, I was endlessly reading research reports, *Barron's* articles, and anything else I could get my hands on so that I could be that much smarter Monday through Friday. But the CFA made that impossible. Ultimately, there are only so many hours in a day.

GETTING BETTER AT YOUR JOB

Studying for the CFA wasn't totally detrimental to my former employers, though. The CFA material was incredibly complementary to the business that we were engaging in every day. Whether it was learning the finer points of equity valuation or understanding how mortgage-backed securities responded to interest rate moves, it was good stuff to know. It made my work, especially my written work, more sophisticated and I think better received by the client base.

The other workplace benefit of studying for the CFA is the ability it gives you to commiserate with your clients. The sell-side is all about building relationships and basically getting people on the buy-side to like you. Well, guess what? Most people on the buy-side have either done the CFA or are doing it. You instantly have something in common with them. This gave me hours of discussion material with clients. They wanted to hear about my experience and I wanted to hear about theirs. Additionally, the sheer fact that I was taking the exams gave me more credibility and—guess what else—yep, respect. Clients respected the fact that I was taking the CFA, and I think they took me that much more seriously as a result.

The way that clients perceive you is critically important in the world of finance. As such, I wouldn't discount the role that Ethics plays in the CFA Program. While many candidates are tempted to think of this material as less important than some of the more quantitative subjects covered in the curriculum, it's clear to me that the CFA Institute is incredibly focused on raising the financial industry's ethical standards.

This is another benefit to the CFA Program, in my opinion. Clients, many of whom have undertaken the CFA journey themselves, understand that CFA charterholders have been extremely well-versed in the realm of Ethics as it relates to finance. It is not surprising that many feel an added level of trust and comfort when dealing with a CFA charterholder.

The bottom line here is that you need to think about your job before you sign on to the CFA Program. Yes, there are some positive impacts, as I've discussed, but you need to be aware that you will physically not be able to put the time and energy into work as you might have done otherwise. Take this into consideration along with the other factors we'll discuss, as it's important to think about the whole picture.

LIFE IS PASSING ME BY

When I entered the CFA Program at age twenty-nine, I was young(ish) and not yet married. But during the period in which I was taking the CFA exams, my life changed drastically. Not only did I get married, but I became a parent as well. Going through the whole process with an extremely supportive partner was a godsend. I truly would not have been able to do it without her, especially as I studied the Level 3 material one final, gut-wrenching time as my baby boy crawled around my feet.

The point is that LIFE doesn't stop and wait for you to complete the CFA Program. So you need to decide exactly which events in your life you are willing to miss out on in order to earn your charter. Let's talk about what this really means on a day-to-day basis.

You will start studying each year in December or January for a test that takes place in June. Now, let's take a collective deep breath and think about the ridiculousness of that statement before moving on. Yes, that's right, you will be studying for six months. What does that mean in reality? Well, the "magic number" is supposedly somewhere between 250-300 hours of study time. I'll let you do your own math on that, but if your numbers work out the same as mine, it basically means that you have to study for fifteen hours per week, EVERY week from January through May. Fifteen hours doesn't sound like much, but believe me, this test will dominate your life.

For me, what it meant was studying every weekend from January until June. I would also study a few weeknights most weeks, but since I worked full-time in a highly demanding job, I could only muster about three hours at most, two or three times a week. Later in the book, I'll provide you with a sample week-by-week study calendar so you can get a visual sense of this endeavor.

Hopefully it's becoming pretty apparent that you won't have time for much else. If you work all day, use half of your weeknights to study, and then study for most of the day on Saturday and Sunday, well, that's pretty much your life.

YOUR BETTER HALF

Realistically, this means that you won't have much time for personal relationships. Managing the relationship with your spouse or significant other throughout this process can be a challenge. I've seen more than one relationship broken up by the process. Hopefully, if you are in a relationship, your partner will be understanding and share your vision for the ultimate goal.

There are some practical ways that you can make your partner feel like you are not ignoring them for six months. Whitney and I started going for long walks during my study breaks or after I was done studying for the day. This gave me a chance to vent about the CFA studying but also to catch up on what was going on with her. Maybe walking isn't your thing but running or biking is more your speed. Find what works for you. This is time that your body and mind need to refresh after the monotony of studying. Getting some quality time in with your spouse as well as exercise is killing two birds with one stone, and when it comes to the CFA, efficient use of time is the name of the game.

THE OFFSPRING

Having kids makes the equation even more complicated. I only studied for one test after becoming a parent, but I can tell you that I have an incredibly high level of respect for anyone who can manage this process with kids. If you want to attempt this as a parent, more power to you, but you must go into it knowing that a) your spouse will probably not be pleased with you, for a period of *years*, and b) you *will* miss some important moments in your child's life, which was even harder for me to accept.

Again, in practical terms, this just means that you'll need to be even more regimented with your time. If you absolutely must attend your son or daughter's recital or soccer game, you'll need to make up those hours at some point. Can you study late at night after they've gone to bed, or does your brain tend to shut off like mine? What about rising before the rest of the family and getting in a few hours before everyone wakes up? You need to figure out what works best for you.

At the end of the day, the ends may justify the means, and of course, people have been sacrificing for the benefit of their kids since the beginning of time, but only you know if that is the right choice for you. My goal is only to make sure you consider these things upfront so that you go into the process eyes wide open.

YOUR MOM IS WORRIED ABOUT YOU!

What about the other people in your life? Mom and Dad? Brothers and sisters? Studying for the CFA exams definitely makes it tricky to find the time to spend with your family.

I was really lucky in that my parents were incredibly supportive throughout the entire process. When I failed tests along the way, I think it affected them more than me. I studied my butt off, did my best on the test, and then accepted the outcome. Well, maybe it wasn't that clean, but you get the idea. My parents took it really hard when I failed. Not because they were disappointed in me, but because they were disappointed *for* me.

Perhaps just as important as their empathy was their understanding that I just wouldn't be around. If they wanted to see me, they had to make the effort. I lived in NYC and Boston at different times in the process, and my parents were about a two-hour drive from either in Connecticut. They'd call and ask if they could make the trek just to have lunch with me, and even then I was sometimes non-committal. I just didn't know if I could spare the time.

What I did know was that I needed to study every Saturday and every Sunday. All day, both days. And sure I'd take some time for lunch, but if my parents were coming, then of course I'd have to clean up the place, figure out what we'd eat, etc. It was just too much to think about. It was MUCH easier just to say, "No, not this weekend" because I didn't feel like I could spare the brainpower if just to think about what we'd eat. What I'm trying to say here is that you will have very real, very rational reasons to not spend even an hour with the people you love and who love you. Thankfully, I have very patient parents who'd deal with the ill-tempered hermit that I had become and come by for an hour or two (eventually smartening up and bringing lunch with them) just to see me and make sure I wasn't "working too hard."

In addition to missing out on several visits from the folks, I also missed holidays, trips to see my in-laws, weddings, graduation parties, etc. You name it, I missed it! Thankfully my family was understanding, and I'm eternally grateful to them for that.

Missing all of these events is not ideal, but it's also not the end of the world. People always have commitments in life—jobs, school, military service, etc.—that many times keep them from spending time with loved ones. The CFA Program is just another version of this.

There are some practical things that you can do to keep up with your extended family during this time. First of all, make use of the off-season. So, for instance, if you're sitting for a June exam, you probably won't be studying July through November. That's a big chunk of the year. Make it a point to spend time with your family during these months. Most people aren't hitting the books too hard yet during the December holiday season either, so that's a great time to catch up with family members before falling off the face of the earth.

Otherwise, keeping in touch on the phone or even using Skype or FaceTime can be a great way to stay connected with the people who love you without having to burn up too much of your study time.

At the end of the day, you just have to remember, your Mom is worried about you! So give her a call now and then to let her know that you're not "working too hard."

JUST A FRIEND

Finally, if you're like me, and your friends are really important to you, you'll also want to think about how this process is going to impact your relationships there as well.

Again, I missed so many events with my friends while studying for the CFA exams. Nights out on the town, sports games, golf, weddings, bachelor parties—I missed them all! It's rough, but the reality is that you just can't do it all, especially if these events are close to exam time. You won't be able to spare the time.

If they're good friends, they'll understand and they'll be ready to get you back once the exam is done with. I'm lucky in that I feel like I can go months without seeing many of my friends, but then we pick right up where we left off the next chance we get.

So, when it comes to keeping up with your friends, you have to pick your spots. The same advice about taking advantage of the "off-season" holds true for friends as well. And even during the exam study period, you should be able to squeak in some friend time if you're smart about it.

While you'll probably be studying both weekend days, getting out with your friends for dinners or drinks can be a really nice distraction. You won't want to go overboard and stay out late or overindulge in the booze, as your motivation to study the next day will evaporate, but a night out can really be a good stress-release.

A LITTLE EFFORT GOES A LONG WAY

Whether it's your spouse, your extended family members, or your friends, you just need to be smart about managing your relationships. It's not natural for many people to think about having to "manage" these relationships, as hopefully most of them are normally effortless. But studying for the CFA exams is a time in your life when you are going to be putting yourself under an abnormal amount of stress. And, of course, you're going to have almost no free time.

In all likelihood, you'll be fine with all of these relationships, but a little extra planning will help you immensely. Just as you will schedule in when you'll be studying Book 1, Book 2, and so on, think about scheduling in a date night with your significant other, a visit from the folks, or a night out with good friends. By organizing your time effectively, you'll feel less stressed and less guilty about ignoring the most important people in your life.

So if you decide to move forward and enter the CFA Program, I think you'd be smart to think about both what is truly motivating you as well as how it might impact other parts of your life, including your career and the relationships with your friends and family. While it's absolutely possible to keep all these balls in the air, you need to be smart about how you do it. A little extra planning goes a long way.

Chapter 2 Checklist:	
☑ **Do:**	☒ **Don't:**
☑ 1) Think seriously about what your motivation for taking these exams really is.	☒ 1) Wait until you are deep into the CFA process before considering what is really driving you to pursue the designation.
☑ 2) Realize that you realistically will not be able to put the same time and effort into your job as you normally would.	☒ 2) Assume that you can study for the CFA exams without it impacting your work.
☑ 3) Come up with smart ways to stay connected with the people closest to you while working your way through the program.	☒ 3) Get stressed out or feel guilty about ignoring your family and friends.

CHAPTER 3:

Best for Your Career: CFA or MBA?

* Kindergarten Banker

* Finance for Life?

* The Street

* The CFA Charter: Golden Goose or Goose Egg?

* MBA: Money Buys . . . Agitation?

* Excuse Me, Will This Be on the Exam?

* Create Your Own Curriculum

* CFA-related Costs

* Mo Money, Mo Problems

* The Takeaway

KINDERGARTEN BANKER

What should I do with my life? It's a big question. People answer it in many ways, and those answers usually involve things like raising a family, pursuing a fulfilling career, and generally finding happiness. A career in finance certainly has the potential to be fulfilling in many ways. While most kids in kindergarten don't say, "I want to be an investment banker when I grow up," the reality is that finance can be intellectually stimulating, exciting, and lucrative.

Someone who decides to pursue a career in finance will, sooner or later, have to decide how far to take his or her education. So what's better—getting an MBA or a CFA? There are pros and cons to both. Both are serious time commitments. Both can be incredibly useful in terms of increasing your knowledge, bolstering your CV, and improving your network. Ultimately, the decision of which one to choose, or whether or not to pursue a career in finance at all, is very personal. In this chapter, I'll try to help you figure out which direction might be right for you.

FINANCE FOR LIFE?

Are you dead-set on a career in finance? This is a pretty key question when it comes to making the decision of whether or not you should commit a not-so-insignificant portion of your life to pursuing your CFA charter or an MBA in finance. I realize that it might be hard, especially if you're in your mid-twenties, to feel ready to commit yourself to something for life.

Finance is certainly not for everyone. Its image, as a career path, has taken a huge hit since the collapse of Lehman Brothers and the financial crisis that went along with it. It's also pretty clear that we have seen a bubble in finance when it comes to the sheer number of young people who were choosing it as their career path.

How can you blame college kids and MBAs for wanting to go into finance when things were so good? Nowhere else could you have made such a large amount of money at such a young age and, in many cases, have a good time doing it.

THE STREET

Now you may arrive on Wall Street, driven by the money or the mystique of it all at first, but later find out that you really enjoy the work itself. I'm not sure I was necessarily drawn to Wall Street by money or power or anything like that. Truthfully, I sort of fell into it and was happy to land *any* job coming out of college. The fact that the work itself turned out to be so intellectually stimulating was really an added bonus. I love to argue, debate, and learn new things. The roles that I performed on Wall Street put me in a position to do just that. I could read about stocks, bonds, currencies, you name it . . . and then debate my theories with other salespeople, my own analysts, and, most importantly, clients.

Maybe arguing or debating is not your thing, but you've been investing in penny stocks since you were seven. While most kids found comfort in a teddy bear or blanket, you held a copy of Peter Lynch's *One Up On Wall Street* close to your heart as you nodded off in your crib. Maybe you're a quant jockey. You majored in math or computer science or quantum physics or something so complex that I probably can't pronounce it. Maybe you were born to build DCF models, to give birth to algorithms, or to crack the codes that the Big Data of markets provide us with.

If so, then Wall Street may just be the place for you. There are a ton of great jobs on Wall Street, and I've seen both introverts and extroverts do very well. If you're not a quant jockey but like the sound of your own voice, you can always go into sales. If you like numbers, but your idea of a good time is being locked away on your own in a dark room, don't worry, they'll find a place for you.

But maybe finance isn't for you. Maybe you are going to hate yourself if you're not adding more social value to the world. Should you be off doing Teach for America or getting clean water to remote parts of Africa? Only you know this.

Believe me, I think it's incredibly important to know yourself. You need to know your strengths and weaknesses. You need to pursue those things that you REALLY enjoy doing. If you don't, you will drive yourself crazy and live a miserable existence until you give in to what you really want. This is not really a book about that, but I would be remiss if I didn't tell you that you need to be introspective when choosing your path.

Finance can also be a tough road. It can be a brutal business. But average salaries on Wall Street are still far and away the best deal going. You can come right out of college and instantly make more money than any of your friends. Granted, you're going to work your tail off and probably be expected to devote yourself ten times more to your job than anyone you know, but by your mid-twenties, rightly or wrongly, you can be making more money than many people ever make in their lifetimes.

Perhaps more important than the money is the experience that working on Wall Street gives you. I'm not necessarily talking about building up your CV so that you can apply to be the next Treasury Secretary after a stint at Goldman. I'm talking about the day-to-day experience of it all.

Just about every day I've had on Wall Street has been exciting in one way or another, especially the time I spent on the Lehman trading floor in New York. I mean, it almost *has* to be thrilling when you're in an environment like that. My days were spent on a trading floor in Times Square that was the size of an entire city block. Needless to say, it was always an amazing flurry of activity. At any given time, I'd look around and, among the sea of thousands, I'd see grown men and women screaming at one another, slamming phones, or waving their hands in a way that would seem ridiculous in almost any other setting. There were flat-screen TVs all around us airing CNBC, tickers on the walls streaming quotes, and a constant cacophony of voices coming over the "hoot" with the latest views on stocks, bonds, currencies, and everything in between. It was an extraordinarily exciting place to be.

How does this relate to the CFA? Well, I think the choice of whether or not to pursue the designation is pretty binary, and it comes down to whether or not you want to pursue a career in finance, or, if you're already on that path, if you want to stick with it. If you are dead-set on finance, if finance is what you've been dreaming about since you were in kindergarten, then the CFA is probably a good path for you. Nowhere else will you get the amount of detailed training that you will from the CFA curriculum. No designation, certificate, or degree is as widely recognized and respected among hedge funds, investment banks, and the like as the CFA charter.

If you're in the not-sure camp, signing up for the CFA Program is a much different proposition. On the one hand, studying for Levels 1 and 2 will help you to figure out pretty quickly just how much you like finance and want to pursue it as a career path. On the other hand, you are potentially wasting time you could be spending pursuing something that you are more passionate about. It takes a long time to become an expert in anything. So the sooner you get started pursuing something that you love, the better.

THE CFA CHARTER: GOLDEN GOOSE OR GOOSE EGG?

So what about the CFA Program? Is it the answer to all of your career hopes and dreams? One private banker I spoke with recently told me: "I am telling every kid coming into the business now to just get started on the CFA. That thing is like a golden ticket. You can do an MBA later if you want, but get that CFA charter ASAP. Even having Level 1 done shows potential employers that you are serious."

So *is* the CFA a golden ticket? In short, no. While I agree with that private banker that taking a level or two of the CFA sends a powerful message to prospective employers, I think that viewing the charter as a golden ticket might only set one up for disappointment.

Perhaps there was a time, probably in the early 2000s, when having your charter was pretty close to gold. I was a pretty junior salesman on Wall Street at the time, and holding a CFA charter was much less prevalent than it is today. Pretty much only sell-side research analysts, buy-side research analysts, and portfolio managers held them. Very occasionally, you'd find a research sales person with their CFA charter, but that was only because they were probably in research before making the switch to sales.

To put it in perspective, in 2012 over 219,000 people registered for the CFA exams.[4] This represents almost three times the approximately 74,000 enrolled in the CFA program back in 2000. Cumulatively, there are now north of 100,000 people globally who lay claim to the title "CFA Charterholder," a number which has more than doubled since the early 2000s.

But these days, even being a charterholder is not a guarantee of employment. There are many more charterholders out there in the world, and you could argue that each incremental person who earns the right to use the "CFA" devalues the distinction to some degree. That said, the fact that so many more people are taking these tests shows you that there is an increasing view that the CFA designation is a must-have credential, and people are willing to sacrifice a great deal to pursue it.

---

[4]The actual number of candidates sitting for exams in 2012 was 168,427. This represents approximately 77% of people who registered for exams that year. This is not an anomaly as every year a similar percentage of candidates do not show up on exam day; presumably this is due to a lack of preparedness. Source: CFA Institute website: www.cfainstitue.org.

When I thought about taking the test back in 2007 and wondered whether or not the CFA charter might become required at some point, I may have been ahead of my time. Certainly, most equity sales people don't have their CFA charters, but it's much more common than it was ten years ago. As for sell-side analysts, buy-side analysts, and portfolio managers? It's pretty much a requirement now, especially if you're just trying to crack into the field. So if any of those paths are attractive to you, you might as well get started with the CFA Program.

Demand for the designation has also broadened out. What was once a designation pretty much concentrated among analysts and portfolio managers has now become a required or at least preferred skill in many other related professions. Look at investment consulting, for instance. Those guys pretty much *have* to be CFA charterholders these days. It's become a requirement in their field. A quick look at the websites of Cambridge Associates or any of the other leading investment consulting firms shows that the CFA Program has become standard operating practice for them.

I think the reason why demand for charterholders has broadened out is the scope of the curriculum. Candidates are tasked with becoming experts in such a wide variety of areas. Everything from how hedge funds calculate performance returns to estimating an emerging market company's weighted average cost of capital. The skills that candidates attain are applicable to a very wide range of professions.

In addition to this broadening out of the demand, it's undeniable that the CFA charter is held in very high esteem by the entire investment industry. In my opinion, there is no question that the CFA charter is the gold standard in the investment world. Sure there are other designations—the CFP®, the CIMA®, and the CAIA®. All of those designations are respectable and they take a lot of hard work to attain. But the CFA charter is the cream of the crop, especially in the investment banking, portfolio management, consulting, and hedge fund worlds.

As the CFA Institute states on their website:

> *The Chartered Financial Analyst® (CFA®) charter is the global investment industry's most challenging and most widely respected graduate-level investment credential.*

I think it's hard to argue with that. You could argue that some of the other designations have more focus on specific areas like private wealth management or alternative investments, which may be true, and is certainly something to consider if those are paths that you are considering, but the CFA charter is absolutely the most prestigious.

Attaining the CFA designation enables you to prove a level of competence without uttering a word. Potential employers will look at your CV and know that you are an expert in the curriculum. That is no small statement. The curriculum is so broad in its scope and dives so deep into so many complicated topics, that potential employers have a really good idea about your investment knowledge level before you even walk in the door. In fact, perhaps the greatest benefit is that the CFA charter gets you in the door in the first place.

Potential employers will not necessarily expect you to be a subject matter expert in any given asset class, but they will know that you've got the academic chops to learn the ins and outs of what it is they do every day. That's important.

The other boon to your career that I'll get into in more detail in the "Life after the CFA" chapter is the CFA network. Just like your undergrad or business school alumni networks, the CFA network can be a great resource. I've found it to be extremely valuable. First of all, you instantaneously have a shared experience with people you might be trying to connect with. How can you not? You have the same battle scars. No one, even those that pass all three levels on their first attempt, makes it through the process unscathed.

The more targeted you get with your CFA network, the more useful it is likely to be. If you're in Cleveland, Ohio, for example, you will find much greater value in networking with the people in the "CFA Society Cleveland" than with the global network of charterholders. This tactic is especially effective in smaller geographic areas, but even in some of the world's larger cities, the credential can help open doors. There are literally CFA societies all over the world, from Atlanta to Austria, Barbados to Beijing, and Calgary to Cyprus. I'd recommend joining and getting involved with your local chapter.

While I may dispute that the CFA charter is a golden ticket, I obviously see a great deal of value coming from it. The networking that your shared experience enables you to do is a prime example, as is the wide variety of professions the CFA Program can prepare you for. And of course, if the words "CFA Charterholder" or "CFA Candidate" on your CV get you in a door that would otherwise have been closed, well then, the network may prove to be more powerful and impactful than all of the investment knowledge you gain along the way.

MBA: MONEY BUYS . . . AGITATION?

So, what about an MBA? Well, to put it bluntly, business school is a huge pain in the neck in some ways, but completely worth it in other ways. First of all, you need to take the GMAT to get into business school. This is basically the SAT all over again. I studied for a few months out of a generic GMAT study guide and ended up scoring reasonably well. I didn't break any world records, but most business schools ask you to aim for 700 (or above) and I was in that neighborhood. It at least put me in the ballpark, and then through a combination of references, work experience, and my written application, I was able to lock up a spot at NYU Stern.

I've always been able to do pretty well on standardized tests when it came to the verbal portion, but the math has always thrown me for a loop. I wound up scoring in the ninety-ninth percentile in verbal and in the fortieth percentile in math. Can someone please remind me how I ended up in finance? I can imagine that many people in finance would have the exact opposite scores as me. And if you're taking any of these tests in a language that is not your first one, then my God, I have a TON of respect for you! These tests are hard enough already. I can't imagine trying to deal with taking them in a foreign language.

Assuming that you do reasonably well on the GMAT, have good references and hopefully some quality work experience, you should be able to find your way into a good business school. Some people argue that if you don't go to a Top 10 business school, then it's not worth going at all. I disagree. There are many more than ten great business schools out there.

Just take a look at job postings at different sell-side and buy-side firms. Even some of the most prestigious firms out there will specify if an MBA and/or CFA is required, but very rarely do they specify a Top 10 MBA. I'm sure those kids are more sought after and might have better companies coming to campus, but the reality is that if you're smart, can represent yourself well in person, and go to a halfway-decent business school, you have just as good a chance at career success as Top 10ers, even if you went to a school outside that range.

It's worth noting that the same material is taught at all of these schools anyhow. You'll probably be reading Harvard Business School case studies about Starbucks and Walmart no matter which school you attend. The only difference is that at XYZ Business School, you most likely won't be getting taught by the professor who actually authored the case. Of course at Harvard you'll probably be taught by that person's TA (teaching assistant) anyhow, so the lower-ranked school can be better in some regards.

EXCUSE ME, WILL THIS BE ON THE EXAM?

So let's talk about what business school is like. In many ways I found it to be much more enjoyable than undergrad. You're older and usually have more real-world experience, which tends to help make discussions more realistic and more meaningful. Of course, it's probably a low hurdle to clear compared to undergrad. While I loved my alma mater, Stonehill College, the reality is that in college you're a kid. If you were anything like me, then your first priority wasn't necessarily academics. My main priority in college: having fun. Academics, needless to say, were WAY down the list.

Despite my non-academic proclivities, I always was pretty good at keeping my grades in an acceptable range. And, thankfully, by the time I reached business school, I'd matured quite a bit, as had my peers. Most of us had some on-the-job experience, which our teachers respected us for. Rather than simply absorbing lessons, we were able to offer informed opinions and perspectives.

Still, as I learned, one downside to an MBA program is that *you don't actually need to know the material.* That's right. You don't.

Let me give you an example. I've always had trouble with Statistics. I struggled through it in college. In grad school, Stats is part of the first-year core classes, like Accounting and other foundational courses. If you don't know, the way that business school works is that you do your core classes in the first year and choose your classes in the second year according to your major or focus.

My Stats teacher at NYU Stern was an absolute rocket scientist when it came to numbers. He was a lovely man, but he was on about level 100, and I was still trying to figure out what game we were playing. Needless to say, when final exam time came around, it wasn't pretty. I wrote down some gibberish and tried to come up with some numbers and equations that might give the impression to whoever happened to grade that mess that I had something more substantial than air between my ears.

I got a 34. That's right, a 34 on my final exam, out of 100. What grade did this ultimately win me in the class? B minus. Yeah, B minus. Many of you overachievers would be mortified with a B minus, but I was over the moon. There was only one problem: I still didn't know the material. And, quite frankly, I was OK with that. I just wanted to be done with Stats forever, and a B minus let me move on. So I passed the class and inched closer to my degree, but I was still horrible at Stats. Incidentally, the CFA was not so forgiving when it came to Stats, but on the bright side, I walked away from the CFA Program actually knowing this subject like the back of my hand.

So, the dirty little secret about business school is that it's nearly impossible to fail. If you show up, at least reasonably often, you're not going to fail. You may not learn everything that you were supposed to learn. But you'll pass. You'll leave with that coveted MBA.

This, of course, is not the same with the CFA Program. For better or for worse, you REALLY have to know the material on the CFA exams. Trust me, I've taken enough of these tests to know that there is no way around it. If there were, I would have found it.

I don't want to come down too hard on MBA programs. The truth is that I learned a great deal as I pursued my degree. I was privileged to learn from some amazingly talented professors who took their job of educating my classmates and me very seriously. My point rather is that the CFA Program is much more black and white. The MBA has a bit more gray area, and that can be good or bad, depending on your perspective.

Another area where perspective matters when it comes to earning an MBA is how the work actually gets done. Business school is group-work central. Some people love this. You get to know your classmates well and get to do some fun projects together. Perhaps if you're in business school full-time, this would be a great way to connect with your peers. Some people thrive on collaboration and love working as a team. But when you are doing your MBA at night like I was, this can be a nightmare, as group-work is generally done outside of the classroom.

In my class, everyone was working full-time, which pretty much meant we'd be spending our weekends together. And the coordination was painful at times. We'd always suffer from too many cooks in the kitchen, or someone wanted to stay until midnight when everyone else wanted to be home for dinner. Usually, the group would divvy up the task into individual parts and then everyone would go their separate ways. Of course, then you risked your project really being some kind of a hodgepodge when it was all put together, but people rarely cared. The goal was to get it done.

The CFA Program, of course, is the opposite situation. It is a self-study program. Sure there are classes and seminars you can attend, but at the end of the day, it comes down to you and the material. I actually liked this as I think I learn best from a book, and I really enjoyed the flexibility that moving at my own pace allowed me.

Classes in business school take place at set times, and if you miss them, you're immediately at a disadvantage. The CFA Program offered considerable flexibility in this regard as, for instance, if I had a particularly busy week at work, I could throttle back on my studies that week and make up for it at my convenience.

CREATE YOUR OWN CURRICULUM

On the positive side for MBA programs, they allow you to pursue your interests and gravitate toward classes and topics that may be a more natural fit for you. I've already made it pretty obvious that I am no quantitative genius, so it's probably not surprising that I took classes like Advanced Negotiations (1 *and* 2). This was basically a class where all you had to do was argue and debate. They'd give you a scenario where a compromise needed to be made, and you'd be set up to negotiate with someone else. You'd have some info and they'd have some info, and the two of you would get together and hash things out until you came to an agreement. You'd usually go off to some corner of the school during class and hammer out your deal, then come back and compare notes with the rest of the class to see who was able to work out the best deal. I loved it.

So, when I could, I took lots of classes that focused on "softer" skills and classes that allowed me to make use of the creative side of my brain, like advertising and marketing. I even took a class on how to launch a hedge fund.

So I really liked the freedom that business school gave me to pursue my areas of interest. The CFA Program doesn't allow you to tailor your education like this.

CFA-RELATED COSTS

When I weigh the positives and negatives, it's clear to me that the CFA Program does have some very real advantages compared to an MBA. My sense is that the CFA designation is better placed than the MBA in the rapidly changing education landscape. There's a great deal of value in the fact that you have to really know the material. And, in my opinion, the prestige of some MBA programs doesn't necessarily translate to career preparation. When it comes to a Top

10 business school MBA, for example, the most impressive thing about it to potential employers *may* be that you were accepted at the school in the first place.

Another major advantage to the CFA Program is that it's not nearly as expensive. Sure you can run up bills of several thousand dollars per year on CFA materials if you go "all in" on study guides, videos, classes, and the like, but that pales in comparison with what you can spend on an MBA, as I'll show you shortly.

The following table provides a sample cost analysis of what a typical Level 1 candidate's expenses might look like.

Sample CFA cost analysis (Level 1)*	
	Estimated Cost
CFA Institute fees	
Program enrollment fee (Level I only)**	$440 – $530
Exam Registration**	$680 – $1,055
CFA Sample exams 2 x $40/each	$80
subtotal	**$1,200 – $1,665**
Third-party costs	
BSAS practice exam***	$149
Schweser Premium Study Package****	$999
Schweser Secret Sauce	$99
Schweser 3-Day Exam Workshop (Classroom)	$499
subtotal	**$1,746**
Other costs	
Calculator (TI BA II Plus or HP 12c)	$60
subtotal	**$60**
Grand total	**$3,006 – $3,471**

*This is meant to give you a general idea of what costs could look like. Actual prices change and you'll tailor your own package as needed.
**The CFA Institute encourages candidates to sign up early. Fees vary depending on when you sign up (early, mid, or late in the process).
***This refers to the Boston Security Analysts Society, who put together an excellent, albeit costly, practice exam.
****I picked Schweser's second costliest package for this analysis, but you may decide to go with a different version depending on your needs.
Source: CFA Institute website, Schweser website, BSAS website

MO MONEY, MO PROBLEMS

So let's say you spend $3200 to take each level of the CFA Program. Now, I haven't included things like buying notebooks or desks or chairs as you'll presumably need those whether you do the CFA or the MBA. So, $3200 x 4 exams (yes, sorry but I am going to assume you fail one along the way!), equals a grand total of $12,800.

Spending over twelve thousand dollars to earn a designation certainly isn't chump change, but it's also nothing compared to the cost of some MBA programs.

A quick side-note to consider is that as a CFA charterholder, you'll need to pay annual dues for the right to use "CFA" after your name. The current annual membership fee is $275. If you are a member of a local CFA Society chapter, that will probably cost another $100 or so on an annual basis. Now break out your TI BA II's and calculate the Time Value of Money on that $375 expenditure over the course of your lifetime. Or not.

Seriously, though, the MBA doesn't have similar *explicit* long-term costs, but they are pretty good at tracking you down to give them donations. So keep that in mind.

How do the MBA numbers stack up in comparison? Well, they're not pretty. The table on the following page shows the costs associated with the full-time MBA programs for the Top 10 rated business schools in the US. I realize that I told you that you don't need to be a Top 10er to be successful, but I've used these schools as the data was readily available, and I'd just like you to get a glimpse of the approximate costs. Just about every business school makes these numbers available on their website, so you can research the school of your choice on your own.

So cost-wise, you are talking about spending twelve or thirteen thousand dollars TOTAL to earn the CFA designation vs. around two hundred thousand dollars (remember the figures on the following page are per year and these programs are two years!) to earn an MBA.

Now granted those MBA costs are really worst-case scenario numbers. You can do it much cheaper. How? Well, you can attend an Executive MBA program, for instance. These programs allow you to continue to work but earn your MBA at night. This is what I did through the Lehman-NYU Stern alliance program. One advantage to this path is that, similar to the CFA, you can continue to progress in your career and earn money while pursuing your degree. The downside is that your golf game will not get as good as the full-time

MBA students and you will probably not go through multiple passports while touring the world's most exotic locations like your full-time counterparts. Am I bitter? Possibly, yes.

		Tuition per year (full-time)	Other costs**	Total per year
	**How costs stack up for the *US News & World Report*'s 2013 Top 10 ranked Business Schools***
#1	Harvard Business School	$56,175	$52,525	$108,700
#1	Stanford University	$59,550	$43,829	$103,370
#3	University of Pennsylvania (Wharton)	$64,828	$32,252	$97,080
#4	MIT (Sloan)	$58,200	$30,749	$88,949
#4	Northwestern University (Kellogg)	$56,550	$27,904	$84,454
#6	University of Chicago (Booth)	$56,000	$32,683	$88,683
#7	University of California Berkeley (Haas)***	$58,284	$24,108	$82,392
#8	Columbia University	$58,384	$32,314	$90,698
#9	Dartmouth College (Tuck)	$58,935	$31,265	$90,200
#10	New York University (Stern)	$56,544	$35,722	$92,266
			Avg annual cost	$92,679

Source: *US News & World Report* website, individual school websites
*Rankings are from the 2013 *US News & World Report*'s "Best Business Schools" list.
**"Other costs" generally includes room & board, books & supplies, health insurance, and other miscellaneous costs.
***I used the "out of state" figures here, and they include health insurance in the tuition. For HBS & Stanford, I took an average of the high and low scenarios shown on their website. When *US News & World Report*'s figures differed from the individual school websites, I went with the individual school's number.

Additionally, you may be able to find MBA programs that are cheaper than the ones I've listed. You need to find the right mix of cost vs. quality and reputation that works for your goals. Also, keep in mind that the prices for tuition and other costs are "list prices," meaning that if you qualify for scholarships or financial aid, the costs may indeed be quite a bit lower for you.

Finally, you should find out which of these costs your employer will pay for (if any). The Great Recession took a bit of a toll on what some companies are willing to pay in terms of tuition and other educational costs, but most firms will still offer *something*.

If the CFA designation is essential to your job, most bulge-bracket investment banks will pay for it. Asset managers offer similar arrangements. When it comes to smaller firms, it's more hit or miss.

The story is similar when it comes to MBA-related costs. I don't often hear of companies that will send you off to full-time business school for two years and foot the bill, but many will at least provide some assistance if you are going to school at night. Make sure to take advantage of these benefits. I was able to earn my MBA from NYU Stern for essentially one quarter of the "list price" by taking advantage of these benefits, and let me tell you, it's a great feeling to graduate without the student loans that most full-time MBA students leave school with. If you can avoid getting into debt, I think that's a great idea.

You might be wondering what the comparable "pot of gold" at the end of the rainbow might be for CFA vs. MBA candidates. To give you some insight, I've reproduced the table below, which is taken (with permission) from Linette Lopez's article "MBA vs. CFA: Here's How To Decide Which One To Get" from BusinessInsider.com.

Degree and Certifications	Median Pay (0-5 YE)	Median Pay (10+ YE)
CFA and No MBA	$72,900	$132,000
CFA and MBA	$87,200	$148,000
MBA and No CFA	$57,700	$105,000
MBA in Finance and No CFA	$63,100	$119,000
* YE = Years of Experience		

Source: Linette Lopez, "MBA VS. CFA: Here's How To Decide Which One To Get," *BusinessInsider.com*, April 30, 2013. Original data via *PayScale*.

As you can see, the CFA appears to command a fairly significant premium to the MBA for those with both very little experience and those with over ten years of experience. The combination, of course, seems to be the best of all.

THE TAKEAWAY

If you're a hundred-percent certain that you love finance and want to become an expert, the CFA designation is an obvious choice. The cost of the program relative to most MBAs is astoundingly low and the payoff seems to be higher.

However, there are risks involved with pursuing a CFA charter. Given the very low pass rates, one can easily make an argument that the MBA is a safer route as it provides you with a much greater chance of actually coming away with a degree.

If you want a broader experience that allows you the potential to move in a variety of directions post-graduation, and the opportunity to refine your "softer skills," the MBA may be the route for you.

If you're a real glutton for punishment like me, you can do both. Or if you just want to say, "Screw the establishment" and go launch the next Google or Facebook in your garage, well then, more power to you!

Chapter 3 Checklist:	
☑ **Do:**	☒ **Don't:**
☑ 1) Think long and hard about whether or not finance is the right career path for you *before* signing up for the CFA Program.	☒ 1) Put an incredible amount of time and effort into something you're not sure is the right path for you.
☑ 2) Realize that the CFA designation has a tremendous amount of positives including the investment knowledge you gain, the self-discipline you learn, and the networking opportunities.	☒ 2) Assume that earning your CFA charter will result in riches and career satisfaction.
☑ 3) Think about the costs of earning an MBA vs. CFA in terms of money and time commitments.	☒ 3) Automatically assume that an MBA or CFA is the right choice for you without a thorough investigation of all of the pros and cons.
☑ 4) Find out if your employer will finance the costs associated with pursuing an MBA or CFA.	☒ 4) Pay for the entire cost of the CFA Program and/or third-party study packages before checking on the benefits your employer might provide in this area.

CHAPTER 4:

Before You Crack the Books

* Getting Started
* Ignore at Your Peril
* Get Comfortable, We're Going to Be Here Awhile
  + Away Game
  + Home Court Advantage (and Disadvantage)
* Keep Their Heads Ringing
* Virtual Insanity
* Sounds Like a Setup to Me
* Be Nice to Your Body

GETTING STARTED

So let's say you've made up your mind and have decided to enter the CFA Program. I feel really bad for you. I mean . . . congratulations! Such wonderful experiences lie ahead! Seriously, though, once you've made the decision to start this journey, there are some basic things you need to do.

Probably first and foremost you should check out the CFA Institute website: www.cfainstitute.org to familiarize yourself with the requirements of the program, timelines, associated costs, and almost every other detail you can think of.

You're obviously going to have to sign up for the program, but before signing up and entering your credit card details on the CFA Institute's website, I'd advise you to have a chat with your employer. As I've mentioned, many employers will provide you with financial assistance when it comes to the CFA, so if there are benefits that may be available to you, you might want to look into them.

Along these lines, speaking to your employer ahead of time can be beneficial because they may have certain rules that you need to follow in order to get reimbursed or for them to pay for the cost of the program upfront.

Additionally, your employer may have a preferred third-party study note provider that they receive discounted materials from. I used Schweser products in my preparations, but your employer may have a contract with 7city®, for instance, and it therefore might be a better deal for you to use them.

If your employer does not have a provider that they prefer, then I'd take a look at the websites of some of the third-party providers such as Schweser and 7city®. See if there is a study package that fits your needs. Do you want live instruction? Do you like flash cards? Is online access important to you? By poking around the websites of these providers, you can get an idea of what is on offer and hopefully find a study package that works for you. The CFA Institute is not going to steer you in any one direction in particular. So this is something you'll need to do on your own.

When should you be doing all of this stuff? Well, you're lucky because Level 1 is offered twice a year these days, once in June and once in December. In my opinion, you'd be wise to sign up for the test at least six months in advance. The earlier you sign up, the cheaper the rates you'll get from the CFA Institute and, of course, the more preparation time you will have.

So I'd probably look to sign up for a June test at least by the end of November—or a December test at least by the end of May. Once you've signed up for the exam and have chosen a third-party provider, there are just a few more things you should think about before cracking those books . . .

IGNORE AT YOUR PERIL

When most people sign up for the CFA exam, they think about how hard it is going to be to master such complicated material—and such a high volume of it. They think about how they will manage their time and commitments. They wonder how they will juggle work, school, family, etc., and still put in the needed hours to master the concepts of the CFA curriculum. But most people don't anticipate the effects that studying for the CFA exam will have on their bodies.

In my experience, you need to get some basic things right before you even think about cracking the books. I'm talking about where you'll study, what your setup will look like, and a million other details that are absolutely essential to (literally) position you for success.

GET COMFORTABLE, WE'RE GOING TO BE HERE AWHILE

Let's start with your physical setup for studying. Where are you going to study? That's a big, big question. You really need to spend some time thinking about it. If you're going to really commit yourself to this beast, you need to set yourself up to succeed, and picking the right place to study is a hugely important part of that.

Think about it. You will spend about three hundred hours per level studying. Now, let's say you only fail one test along the way, which would be quite successful in my opinion; you are still looking at about twelve hundred hours of studying. Just to make the math easy, let's assume you did all of your studying in twelve-hour stretches from 7am-7pm (which of course is unrealistic as you'd need breaks for lunch, etc.). But just to give you an idea, you're looking at about one hundred full days of studying. God, I sometimes get antsy sitting around for half an hour, much less ONE HUNDRED DAYS! And that's if you do well. What happens if it takes you six tries like me?

Even my rudimentary math skills tell me that 6 x 300 = 1800. In twelve-hour increments, you're talking about 150 days! (Ok, you got me, I needed the calculator on that one.) Anyhow, the point is that you are going to be spending a *ton* of time studying, so you better get comfortable.

First and foremost you need somewhere quiet where you won't be disturbed. I was living in NYC when studying for Level 1. Whitney and I shared a one-bedroom apartment at the time. Slight problem with one-bedroom apartments—there's really nowhere to get away. So I had to find a place of my own, which ended up being in the building next door that was owned and operated by the same company. They had a nice study room where I would hole up for hours upon hours. The main problem that I encountered here was that it wasn't quiet enough. It was a public "study" room, but the building was full of families with small children, and inevitably once every hour or so, some kid would burst into the room screaming and completely cause me to lose my train of thought. So, that wasn't ideal but at least it was really convenient. This is another thing to consider. You may love studying at the library or at Starbucks or anywhere else, but make sure that you can get there in less than five minutes. The reason being that you'll want to squeeze every last second you can into the studying before you need to go home, go to work, go to school, etc., and you'll also want to be able to pop over to your study place if you have an extra hour on a weeknight. If it's tough to get to, you won't go.

Away Game

Now what about Starbucks or the library? I've never done particularly well with Starbucks, but a lot of people like it. There is coffee, obviously. That's a plus for those who benefit from caffeinating themselves, and they usually have Wi-Fi, which is a double-edged sword in my opinion but certainly useful if you're making use of online study resources. My problem with Starbucks and even the library is that I'm too darn curious about other people. Studying for the CFA is largely a solo project. It's you and the material, and the two of you better get to know each other very well. At Starbucks, there's the talkative girl or interesting-looking guy at the next table. Is he or she starting the next Apple or Google from their laptop right here in this Starbucks? Should I say screw this CFA stuff and get in on the ground floor? Is that creepy old guy staring at me for any reason in particular? Do those teenagers HAVE to be screaming at the top of their lungs?

Too many distractions! Way too many.

Bottom line: Set yourself up to succeed, not to fail, by studying in the place that's right for you. If you must study in a Starbucks, see if you can find a small table away from everything else that faces a wall. If you can't see other people, they'll be less distracting. Same thing with the library. Find some nook or cranny that is off the beaten path where you'd really have to strain your neck to get a glimpse of another human. If you're in a place where all you have to do is look up from your book to see a beehive of human activity, then you're in the wrong place if you're prone to distractions like me.

Home Court Advantage (and Disadvantage)

What about studying at home? Let's assume that you have the good fortune of having a second bedroom or office or some other area where you can hide away and study. That's great, because nothing is more convenient than being at home. However, there are a few problems. Willpower is one. When you're at the library, you're kind of stuck there. Unless you decide to dive into a copy of *War and Peace* or take a nap, you're there to study.

At home you need to exercise willpower. I'm a guy, and like most guys I like sports. So when there was a big game on (or games— hello, March Madness!), it was more difficult to stay disciplined. Fortunately, I quickly learned the ways of DVR, so I could watch my teams play when it was convenient for me, which was typically after destroying my brain with bland material for a few hours. If sports aren't your thing, then there is inevitably something else to distract you from studying at home. Maybe it's surfing the Internet, maybe it's chatting on the phone, or maybe it's just taking a nap.

Additionally, unless you live by yourself, you've got other people who can potentially distract you at home. Now, I wouldn't necessarily start referring to those you live with as "distractions" as it may result in you not living with them anymore, but rather just be cognizant of the realities of living with other people. If you have a roommate or two, go into it realistically knowing that there are going to be many times when it's just not quiet enough at home and you're going to need to escape to somewhere nearby to study.

The same goes if you are married or live with a significant other. Kids, of course, take this all to a whole other level. Studying with kids in the house is really difficult. One problem is the noise. Kids make noise, and depending on their age, it's difficult if not impossible to ask them to be quiet. The other thing is that, as a parent, you'll likely feel guilty about ignoring them. You don't want to be the grump who just wants quiet with little kids who just want to spend time with their mom or dad. Basically, it's a rough situation, and one that's best avoided if you can.

One thing that is essential, if you decide to go the home route, is a door. You need the office or bedroom or wherever you are studying to have a door so that you can close yourself off from the world and not hear a peep. Even with a door, you still may need something for your ears.

KEEP THEIR HEADS RINGING

Earplugs can be invaluable wherever you study. I used earplugs for most of my time studying and then used them at the actual exams themselves. I think most people use them during the exams. I usually went with the clear rubbery kind that you can find at any drugstore.

I think they are swimmers' earplugs. You can mold them to the inside of your ears so you can really make sure you can't hear. I tried a few different kinds over the years but the clear rubbery ones are the best, in my opinion. I even got to the point where I was sleeping with them as our apartment building was noisy sometimes and I needed the sleep (especially on nights before the exam).

Another option is music. Now, I didn't really go with this option for most of my time studying for these tests as I found it too distracting. I would put some music on and start to study but then I'd realize that I was focusing on the lyrics rather than the material, which was completely the opposite of what I was trying to do. That changed on my final exam.

Yes, for my third (gasp) attempt at Level 3, I used music. In fact, I went out and bought myself some of those really badass rapper-style Dre Beats headphones. Because obviously nothing is more hardcore than studying for the CFA, right? So did I listen to some hardcore beats or maybe some nineties gangsta rap in honor of Snoop and Dre? Well, not exactly. I went with the classics . . . as in classical music. I found this album on iTunes called *Exam Study Classical Music to Increase Brain Power*. Pretty hardcore, right?

Well, it did what I wanted it to do. I was breaking some of my own advice in that I was studying at home, and while I had a nice office to study in (we'd moved to the suburbs of Boston by this time), I had no door on my office. This would have been a big enough problem if I were only hearing my wife entertain herself with that classic American TV show *Gossip Girl*, but by this time I had a son as well. Yep, little Charlie was starting to crawl around and was certainly old enough to make LOTS of noise.

So the classical music in the Dre Beats headphones was a godsend. It blocked out the noise, was actually quite soothing to listen to, and most importantly I was not distracted by the music. Obviously, there are no words, so you're not thinking lyrics in your head, just melodies. I'm no expert in what music does to your brain, but I swear that music helped the material to settle into my brain in ways that it otherwise would not have.

Long story short: find a quiet place where you won't be distracted. Get some headphones made by a great nineties rapper and fire up the classical music. If you don't learn the CFA material, at least you'll be able to impress your friends by cleaning up at *JEOPARDY!* when the category is Bach or Mozart.

VIRTUAL INSANITY

When you're studying, you really need to cut yourself off not only from physical distractions but also from virtual ones. This means that you pretty much need to divorce yourself from your phone, tablet, or laptop. It's really tough to grasp a complicated subject if you are taking breaks to check emails, tweets, or Facebook.

Your brain is trying to grasp something that may take the authors of the material twenty or thirty pages to describe. You need to stay with them. Much of the material you will encounter, particularly when you are addressing some of the more complicated subjects throughout the curriculum, like Swaps and Pension Accounting, is cumulative. You need to grasp concept A before moving on to concept B. Not only do you need to grasp concept A, but it needs to be readily accessible when you are trying to grasp concept B. So if you read through concept A and understand it, but then take a break to check Facebook before moving onto concept B, there's a very good chance that your brain will not have concept A readily accessible when you need it. This means you'll have to start over.

I know, it's a frustrating process, and many times I would have to read the same material over and over and over again before understanding the concepts. If you are interrupted during this intense learning phase, it will make your task infinitely more difficult.

I'm realistic. I know that you are not going to completely cut yourself off from the outside world. But I also know that there are times when you get so bored with the material or when your brain is completely fried that you are just looking for a distraction. If your phone is in reach, you'll check it. You'll check email, Facebook, Twitter . . . whatever. Because even a post about the bathroom habits of the children of your "good buddy" that you haven't seen since fifth grade makes for thrilling reading material compared to the intricacies of swaps.

So what to do? Figure out what works best for you. Try turning off your phone. I know. Sacrilege, right? Or at least don't have your phone within reach. My last time through, I kept my phone in the kitchen while I studied in the office. About every hour or two, I'd get up to stretch and check my email. I wouldn't go on Facebook or Twitter as they were just too distracting and I could always catch up later on the happenings on those sites. Checking email was fine because I could respond to a message if someone really needed me or at least prove to myself that nothing was really going on that couldn't be dealt with later. So do yourself a favor and disconnect from the virtual world as much as humanly possible as you study. This is essential to allow your brain a chance to do the really heavy lifting when it comes to grasping tough concepts.

SOUNDS LIKE A SETUP TO ME

What about your actual physical setup for studying? Pretty simple, right? You need a chair and then some kind of a desk or table and you're good to go, right? Well, let's think once more about the sheer number of hours that you are going to spend in the studying position. Nowhere in the CFA curriculum or study guides do they talk about the physicality of studying. Sure, they tell you to get a good night's sleep before the exam and somewhere in there they might even tell you to take a fifteen-minute walk during the break between the morning and afternoon sessions. But what about the long haul? You are going to be sitting on your butt a lot! If you sit most of the time at work, you're only going to be sitting that much more!

I was working on Wall Street at the time I was studying, and while being in sales allowed me to get up and go to a decent amount of meetings, etc., I'd say ninety percent of my work time was still spent sitting.

I'd sit for twelve hours each day at work. Then I'd come home and either a) sit and study for three hours or b) sit and watch TV. Maybe I'd go to the gym for thirty minutes or an hour if I could find the time, but still that's a lot of sitting. The real killer was the weekend. Most people are used to being more active on the weekends. You're going to the park, or playing a sport, or walking around town, or SOMETHING other than just sitting. Studying for the CFA screws up this routine. You now need to sit and study for long stretches on the weekends. If you're not careful, you can basically be sitting nonstop for six months.

BE NICE TO YOUR BODY

I'm no doctor, but all it takes is a simple Google search on the dangers of sitting too much to realize that it messes with you physically. In addition to just generally getting out of shape, the extreme amount of sitting can really mess up your back.

So, what can you do about this? First of all, take breaks. Every hour or two, get up and walk around. As discussed, you may want to take this chance to answer emails, call your mom, or whatever else you need to do. Walk around a bit. Get the blood flowing. Get your heart going a little bit. It's good for you. There's a reason they tell you to get up and walk around on long flights. Maybe you're not at high risk for blood clots, but if you spend several years sitting on your butt, it will age you, and your body will tell you it's not happy.

How do I know? Because my body was kind enough to let me know! I have never felt worse physically in my life than when I was studying for the CFA. In fact, I struggled with serious back pain as I got deeper and deeper into studying for these exams.

So what can you do to avoid all of this sitting? You might try a standing desk, an option that's becoming more and more popular. I've even seen treadmill desks, which allow you to get a bit of exercise in while studying, but admittedly, this would probably be a serious investment for a home office.

Sitting on an inflatable rubber ball is another option. I used one to some extent studying for Levels 2 and 3. It's a good option for people who like a little motion and balance in their seating situation. I didn't fall in love with it, but it may have helped with strengthening or at least stretching the core out. Other options include trying to build some regular exercise into your schedule. Even if it is just thirty minutes a few times per week, I think it will help immensely. Running, lifting weights, doing yoga—really anything that allows you to get off your butt, move, and stop thinking about the CFA for a little while—will do wonders for your mental and physical well-being.

One of the main problems of sitting so much, as I mentioned, is that it screws up your back. I developed some really annoying back problems during my time studying, including a painful herniated disc, and I'm convinced that it was all due to the extreme amount of sitting. The relentless weekday and weekend sitting is just really tough on the back.

Trust me, you really don't want to be dealing with a painful injury while studying. You just don't need the distraction. For me, I think I developed these back problems because I was spending so much time in a hunched-over position. I would sit in the chair at my desk for hours and hours with my body hunched over and my neck bent such that I was staring at a book that was lying flat on the desk. Ultimately, I decided that I needed to rig something up so that I could sit in my chair but look straight ahead. I figured this would put less stress on my neck and back. I needed something that basically placed the book level with my eyes (sort of like a computer) so that I wouldn't be in this unnatural hunched-over position as much.

I searched online and found the Atlas Ultra Ergonomic Book Holder, which looks like this:

Used with permission from Atlas Ergonomic Book and
Copy Holders. www.bookandcopyholders.com

It's something that you might see a Bible sitting on in a church. I used it with the *SchweserNotes*™ and it worked really well. I'm pretty darn sure it helped with the herniated disc as well, which healed up on its own without surgery. This book holder cost me about sixty-five dollars, and I think that it materially improved my life . . . or at least my ergonomics.

The other thing ergonomically that you want to think about is what kind of chair you are going to sit in. Not to belabor the point, but you are going to be spending a ton of hours in this chair, so you need to think about your comfort and your health. I know there are some twenty-somethings probably reading this and thinking, "Seriously? You're telling me to worry about my HEALTH when picking a chair?" Yes, I am. You might as well figure this stuff out now because if you don't, by the time you finish studying for the CFA, you'll be a certified expert in back pain.

I bought a chair called the Boss Black LeatherPlus Executive Chair. It looks like this:

Used with permission from Norstar / dba Boss Office Products. www.bosschair.com

It cost about $170 on Amazon and had good reviews about comfort and ergonomic support. It also is a pretty good-looking chair if I don't say so myself, and much, much cheaper than some things out there. You can easily spend thousands and thousands of dollars on chairs like this, but if you're looking for a cheap option that works, I'd recommend this one. I'm not an expert on ergonomics, but sites like Amazon provide you with tons of customer reviews that can give you an idea for what people who bought the product think of it, and that's how I decided to go with this chair.

So once I got set up with the chair, the book holder, the classical music, and the quiet space, I was pretty much set. Don't get me wrong, I don't think I actually had this setup together until my second or third attempt at Level 3. Learning what works for you is sometimes a gradual process, but pay attention to any warning signs your body is sending you. Don't wait for chronic back pain or other physical issues before making a change.

Simply put, I would advise you not to underestimate the power of having the right setup. The CFA is tough, really tough. And it's tough when absolutely nothing on earth is distracting you, when it's just you and the books. But if you add in screaming kids, a noisy restaurant, or an aching back, it can become downright impossible. Set yourself up to succeed by taking this stuff seriously and put the proper amount of time and effort into setting up your perfect study oasis. This is great stuff to do in the "off-season." In November or December before you start *really* studying for that June test, plan these things out. I promise that you will not regret it.

Chapter 4 Checklist:	
☑ **Do:**	☒ **Don't:**
☑ 1) Spend time in the "off-season" setting up your perfect study oasis.	☒ 1) Think "I can just study wherever," or you'll do yourself an injustice.
☑ 2) Cut yourself off from virtual distractions as much as possible while studying.	☒ 2) Constantly check email, Facebook, Twitter, etc., or your brain won't have a chance to digest some of the deeper concepts.
☑ 3) Pay attention to your ergonomics as well as your eating and sleeping habits.	☒ 3) Let your health deteriorate while you study for six months.

CHAPTER 5:

Level 1

* Cracking the Books
* Unopened Boxes
* Time Is On Your Side (If You Plan Wisely)
  + Week-by-Week Study Plan
  + Crunch Time
  + Exam Day
* Insomnia
* Paradise City
* Don't Be an Idiot
* Irrational Exuberance
* One Down, Two to Go

CRACKING THE BOOKS

Let me just say upfront that my intention with this book is not to go through the specifics of the CFA curriculum with you. You've got enough resources to help you understand the material on the exam, including third-party study notes, videos, seminars, flash cards, etc., not to mention the CFA curriculum itself.

If you're less familiar with the material that is actually covered throughout the CFA curriculum, the table below gives you a nice level-by-level breakdown. This should be treated as a guide to give you a ballpark estimate of the topics covered on each level. Exact weightings change from year to year, and new material is regularly added to and taken away from the curriculum.

Topic Area	Level I	Level II	Level III
Ethical and Professional Standards	**15**	**10**	**10**
Quantitative Methods	12	5-10	0
Economics	10	5-10	0
Financial Reporting and Analysis	20	15-25	0
Corporate Finance	8	5-15	0
Investment Tools	**50**	**30-60**	**0**
Equity Investments	10	20-30	5-15
Fixed Income Investments	12	5-15	10-20
Derivatives	5	5-15	5-15
Alternative Investments	3	5-15	5-15
Asset Valuation	**30**	**35-75**	**35-45**
Portfolio Management and Wealth Planning	**5**	**5-15**	**45-55**
Total	100	100	100

Source: Nancy Regan, *The Gold Standard: A Fifty-Year History of the CFA Charter* (China: BW&A Books, Inc., 2012).

The good news is that Level 1 is like every test you've ever taken in college. You can memorize your way through it. This is probably not something that anyone is going to advertise too broadly to you, but it's true. You can see from the table above that Level 1 is very broad in terms of its scope but not terribly deep in terms how complicated the concepts get. Sure, there are some basic calculations, but essentially the material can be memorized. I was able to pass this test on the first try (no small feat for someone who has failed so many CFA exams!) and I studied like I studied for every other test I'd ever taken.

I took tons of notes and re-read the *SchweserNotes*™ over and over again. When I say that I took tons of notes, I mean TONS. I've always learned by writing. So believe it or not, I basically re-wrote the entire Schweser Level 1 notes multiple times in my own notebooks. That's right. I *literally* re-wrote the *SchweserNotes*™ in my notebook, almost verbatim. I'm sure there is some truth to this method working, but it's obviously also incredibly inefficient. Unfortunately, this method would ultimately lose its effectiveness beyond Level 1 due to the sheer volume of complicated material that needed to be mastered. I would be forced to find another way.

But I felt like I was in decent shape heading into the Level 1 exam in December 2007, fresh off earning my MBA in Finance that September. Did the MBA knowledge help me? Eh, debatable. I'm sure having some (very slight!) knowledge of Statistics and different capital markets concepts helped, but one thing you learn quickly in prepping for the CFA exam is that you have to learn things the "CFA way." The CFA curriculum is different from anything else you have ever studied because they have very specific things they want you to know and very specific ways they want you to know them.

Could someone who is an expert in capital markets pass the three levels of the CFA without studying one word from the curriculum or third-party notes? Absolutely not, in my opinion. I would hear stories from time to time about "a guy I used to work with knew this guy" who just showed up and passed all three exams. Forgive my language but . . . bullsh*t. Produce this person, please. I'd love to interrogate them. Absolutely impossible. I say this not because I am bitter that I took six CFA exams (ok, maybe just a little bit) but because the CFA Institute asks you to learn very precise concepts in a very precise way. Your general knowledge, even if it is expert knowledge, is not enough to get you by.

UNOPENED BOXES

As I've mentioned, Level 1 is the only level you can memorize your way through, and it can be done. How did I do it? I used the *Schweser-Notes*™ and didn't even crack open the curriculum. That's right, the curriculum literally sat in my apartment in an unopened cardboard box and I never even took a look at it. This was because a) I didn't think I needed to look at it, b) the sheer volume of information in the *SchweserNotes*™ was such that I just couldn't fathom more than doubling it, and c) I thought Schweser did a pretty good job of explaining everything.

Did this work for other levels? No. It wasn't until I ultimately changed the way I studied (which I'll discuss more later), and made more time to peruse the curriculum, that I mastered Levels 2 and 3.

Let me be very clear. In no way am I advising you to ignore the curriculum. It is a great tool and, as we'll discuss later, there are some ways that you can be smart about using it. In hindsight, I would have used the curriculum for Level 1 as an additional resource, and I was probably lucky to get by without it.

The curriculum is incredibly robust. There is clearly an amazing amount of time and effort that goes into producing it. My problem is that I have a difficult time getting through such high volumes of information. I'm not the fastest reader in the world. When I read a book, I like to savor each page. So I was really intimidated by the size of the curriculum. These monstrous books with small print show up on your doorstep and you think, "Are these guys serious?"

Of course, the decision to use the curriculum or not is personal and depends on your learning style. As I mentioned, I started using the curriculum in later levels. It's entirely possible that I would have earned my charter much sooner had I tackled the curriculum earlier on in the process.

But generally I found the *SchweserNotes*™ to be a great tool for Level 1. I found them to be readable and easier to digest than the curriculum. The End of Chapter questions definitely helped prepare me for the exams. I absolutely loved the *Secret Sauce*® books that they publish as well, which are basically *CliffsNotes*® for the CFA exams. They do a great job of summing up the material in a relatively compact format that is easy to take with you anywhere for those times when you've got a few spare minutes on your hands.

Ultimately, I think the best method is to use third-party notes as well as the curriculum. But the key, as I ultimately would learn, to passing these exams (especially Levels 2 and 3) is just to take a TON of tests. Schweser tests, CFA tests, mock exams, sample exams, you name it . . . basically anything you can get your hands on.

Make sure you do all of the End of Chapter questions in the *SchweserNotes*™ MULTIPLE TIMES. The End of Chapter questions in the curriculum are also a great tool. Even if you decide that you are absolutely too overwhelmed by the amount of material to even think about using the curriculum, do yourself a favor, crack open that cardboard box, and AT LEAST do the End of Chapter questions. I think you'll find them really beneficial.

And then it's all about hitting the tests. I'll talk more specifics about tests later, but probably the most important thing you can take away from reading this book is the importance of taking practice exams. I think actually taking these tests trumps any and all other forms of preparation.

The good news is that you *can* get through this. Level 1 is your first foray into CFA Land. Most people will tell you that it is the easiest of the three levels, and I would agree with that statement. I think Level 1 covers such a broad scope of material that it really sets the stage for you to dive deeper into the concepts in Levels 2 and 3.

But perhaps most importantly, Level 1 is about learning *how* to study for these tests. What I mean is that very few candidates have ever had to study for anything for *six months* before. It is a new experience. There simply is no way to pass without putting in the time. The conventional wisdom is that it takes 250-300 hours per level. As you'll see in the next section, you need to plan that time wisely.

They have the Internet on *computers* now?

When I started the CFA Program back in 2007, the online options were frankly quite limited. But, like everything else in the world, the CFA learning process is becoming more interactive and more mobile. Here is my advice for taking advantage of the online resources available to you.

1. **Make use of the CFA Institute's website.** There's nothing quite like getting your information directly from the official source. The CFA Institute has done a great job bolstering their website in recent years. The sample exams, mock exams, and access to past years' actual exams (for Level 3) are invaluable.

2. **Make use of third-party provider websites.** I used Schweser and generally found that they've done a nice job improving their online offerings as well. Question banks, online video courses, and other resources are tools that you should definitely consider using. Other third-party providers include 7city® and Stalla®, among others.

3. **Chat rooms/Message boards:** My go-to website was analystforum.com. They've got chat boards for each level and useful tips from other candidates. Just be careful that you don't let other people psych you out (as in "That test was easy!" or "I've already gone through the curriculum three times!") and obviously *do not* post specifics about what was on the actual exam. The CFA Institute is always on the lookout for this type of thing, and it's a great way to get yourself in trouble.

4. **Blogs:** CFA-dedicated blogs are a fairly recent phenomenon, but the team behind the site 300hours.com is doing a nice job compiling useful tips and info from candidates and charterholders. Definitely worth checking out.

5. **Twitter:** Some of the sites mentioned above have their own Twitter feeds as well, which can be helpful in terms of steering you toward their sites when new blog posts are published. I have also created a Twitter feed for this book: **@CFAConfidential** where I intend to share helpful CFA tips, stories, and nuggets of (hopefully) useful information.

TIME IS ON YOUR SIDE (IF YOU PLAN WISELY)

Something that I think is of the utmost importance, no matter what level you are taking, is time management. I'm not talking about managing your time on the exams—if you take enough tests in your preparation, you will learn how to pace yourself. I'm talking about managing your time from December until June.

Level 1 is all about being organized. You will encounter much more difficult material in Levels 2 and 3, but one of the most important things you learn from Level 1 is how to organize your calendar to allow you to actually study for a test for six months—and do so efficiently.

In no uncertain terms, the way that you organize your time will have a significant impact on whether or not you are ultimately successful.

My process every year went something like this: I would begin sometime in November. I wouldn't do much before December, but I'd start to clear the cobwebs out, get my physical study area prepared (clean out things I no longer needed, make sure I had all my materials, etc.), and then I'd generally try to look at some material to refresh my mind a bit. If I was taking a new level, I'd scan through the *SchweserNotes*™ and possibly the refresher books from the last level. If I was taking the same level over again, I'd read Schweser's *Secret Sauce®* for that level to refresh my mind on what material was covered.

After this, I'd lay out my plan for the rest of the time. I used the Calendar application on my Mac, and basically I'd plot out the next five or six months and how I'd spend every week. Generally, if I could figure out a way to make it work cleanly, I'd aim to spend two and a half to three weeks per Schweser book on my initial read through material. With five books, this equates to fifteen weeks. Each Schweser book is set up to roughly match the place you'll find the same concepts in the curriculum.

For instance, in my last go-round at Level 3, the *SchweserNotes*™ were set up as follows:

Book 1: Ethics, Behavioral Finance, & Private Wealth
    Management
Book 2: Institutional Investors, Capital Markets, Economics,
    & Asset Allocation
Book 3: Fixed Income Portfolio Management & Derivatives,
    Equity Portfolio Management
Book 4: Alternative Investments, Risk Management, &
    Derivatives
Book 5: Evaluation, Monitoring, & Rebalancing;
    Attribution, & GIPS®[5]

---

[5]GIPS® refers to the Global Investment Performance Standards—this is essentially a set of very explicit rules for how asset managers should calculate and present their performance. It's more complicated than it sounds!

The curriculum also had five books (though I understand they are now transitioning to six), which were roughly ordered the same way in terms of the material.

So let's say you started in mid-December, then this will take you to around the middle of March, give or take a week depending on your specific plan. During this initial phase, you'll need to dive deeply into the material in each book and go through all of the End of Chapter questions. I would spend both weekend days studying the material and then try to tack on one or two weeknights each week.

By the middle of March, you'll have two and a half months until exam day. From here, I would make a six- to seven-week plan to basically go through all of the material again. During this stage, I'd recommend approximately ten days per book. Obviously, if you're really comfortable with Ethics or something else, you can spend less time there and more time on some of the more complicated material, but an average of ten days per book is about right. During this time, you'll want to re-read the material, which will hopefully be easier the second time through. You'll focus on particularly difficult concepts that you had a hard time grasping at first. You'll do all of the End of Chapter questions again, along with the sample questions provided in the middle of the Schweser chapters. You'll make notes of particular problems or sections of the curriculum where you are having trouble.

Below is a visual representation of how a sample calendar might be structured that is applicable to all three levels:

Week-by-Week Study Plan

November: Housekeeping time

- ▶ Make sure you've got the right books you need
  - ▷ CFA curriculum
  - ▷ Third-party study books
- ▶ Work on your study setup
  - ▷ Where will you study?
  - ▷ What does your physical setup look like?
- ▶ Plan your time
  - ▷ Set up a week-by-week plan that you can stick to

December: Easing into it . . .

- ▶ Week 1: Crack open the books
  - ▷ Take a casual skim through to get an idea of the material
  - ▷ If it's your second attempt at a level, review past notes
    - ▶ The prior year's Schweser's *Secret Sauce®* is a great tool
- ▶ Weeks 2 to 4: Get *something* done
  - ▷ I'd usually tackle *at least* Ethics in December to get it out of the way
  - ▷ But I'd recommend trying to **get through all of Book 1** (of the *SchweserNotes™*) this month

January: Get after it!

- ▶ Kick off your weekly routine in earnest with Book 2 just after New Year's*
  - ▷ For me this meant both weekend days and two to three weeknights per week
- ▶ January 20th: Finish first run through Book 2

February: Getting into the thick of it

- ▶ February 6th: Finish first run through Book 3
- ▶ February 24th: Finish first run through Book 4
- ▶ Weekend away?
  - ▷ Now might be your last chance to get away for a weekend
  - ▷ Go somewhere warm (but bring your books) and relax
    - ▶ Get some work done but realize it won't be full productivity, so factor that into your planning

March: This test is creeping up on you!

- ▶ March 15th: Finish first run through Book 5
- ▶ Now it's time for review, approximately ten days per book**
  - ▷ March 16th—26th: Book 1
  - ▷ March 27th—April 6th: Book 2

---

*Try to average 2.5 weeks per book on the first run-through depending on how weekends fall. This includes doing all End of Chapter questions in the *SchweserNotes™*.
**Try to average ten days per book on the second time through the material. This includes doing all End of Chapter questions *again*.

April: You should be starting to feel like you know a few things by now!

- ► More review
  - ▷ April 7th—17th: Book 3
  - ▷ April 18th—28th: Book 4

May: Crunch time***

- ► Finish review
  - ▷ April 29th—May 8th: Book 5
- ► And now tests, lots of tests
  - ▷ Week of May 9th:
    - ► 2 full Schweser exams
    - ► 1 CFA Sample exam
    - ► 6—10 hours of *SchweserPro*™ QBank
    - ► 6—10 hours of End of Chapter questions (in the curriculum)****
  - ▷ Week of May 16th:
    - ► 2 full Schweser exams
    - ► 1 CFA Sample exam
    - ► 6—10 hours of *SchweserPro*™ QBank
    - ► 6—10 hours of End of Chapter questions (in the curriculum)
  - ▷ Week of May 23rd:
    - ► 2 full Schweser exams
    - ► 2 past-year actual exams (if Level 3)*****
    - ► 1 third-party exam (BSAS, etc.)
    - ► 6—10 hours of End of Chapter questions (in the curriculum)
  - ▷ Week of May 30th:
    - ► 3 past-year exams (if Level 3)
    - ► 1 CFA mock exam
    - ► Review formulas
    - ► Go back to particularly troublesome areas and do more questions in these areas

---

***All dates cited are approximate. They will depend on how fast you're moving and how weekends fall. But the key is to stick to a well-defined schedule.
****Notice I am not cracking the curriculum until May in this sample calendar. This is absolutely a personal decision, but ignoring it completely may not be the wisest decision.
*****The CFA Institute makes several past years' morning exams available for Level 3.

► Last day:
  ■ Review formulas, review problems that you've struggled with, and attempt to do a few of them.

  ■ Rest. You've done enough. Make sure your body is in good shape going into the test.
▷ June 7th (Always first Saturday in June): EXAM DAY!

Crunch Time

I *highly* recommend getting through the material twice by the beginning of May. The last four weeks are not a time to be reading material for the first or even second time. This time is for taking tests. I absolutely cannot overstate how important this is.

What is the right number of tests to take? I'd say the more, the better. I would usually take all six full Schweser exams to start. This typically means an entire day per test. Three hours in the morning, then lunch, then three hours in the afternoon, and then you correct it in the evening. I would get my hands on every past CFA exam (Level 3 only), mock exam, practice exam, and online sample exam I could. This came out to about eight to ten full tests, in addition to the Schweser exams. Take them all. Tests that actually come from the CFA Institute are the most important, especially past exams. I tried to get ahold of every exam that the CFA Institute put out for the last five to seven years. I'm talking not only about recent exams (which, for Level 3, the CFA Institute generally makes available for a few years after the fact) but older exams, too (no longer provided by the CFA Institute but still floating around), as well as past years' CFA mock exams.

I know it sounds crazy to seek out so many exams. But in my experience, it's the only real way to pass these tests. While tweaks are made to the material in the curriculum every year, there are only so many ways they can ask different questions. Seeing how they tested material either in actual exams or mock exams in the past will really help you to understand how they might test it going forward. So, take every test that you have immediate access to, and then go beyond that to leverage your network of fellow CFA candidates to track down past tests. Between myself and one or two colleagues, we were able to track down multiple years of old exams that were no longer published. Finding these may be getting easier with the growth of chat rooms, blogs, and the like. It's worth your time to ask around for them. And don't call me, because I have long since disposed of them!

So, the month of May is all about practice tests. You'll note that you simply do not have enough weekend days (assuming that you work) to take all of the tests. You will almost surely need to take time off from work. I'd suggest trying to tack on a Friday or Monday to a weekend in late April or early May, or both. Then you're going to need to take *at least* a week off prior to the exam itself. You can probably get away with a little less time off for Level 1, but when it comes to Levels 2 and 3, I would not mess around. Take the time. You'll need it.

I would basically take tests every weekend day in May, and then I'd take off from work a few Fridays and Mondays here and there so that I could do a three- or four-day practice test marathon and knock out several at a time. Then, on weeknights, I'd make use of some of the available online tools such as the *SchweserPro*™ QBank, which is a great tool that allows you to generate online tests for yourself and customize them so that you can focus on areas of weakness. I'd take two or three weeknights every week in May and blow through about three hours of these types of questions.

The last week, which I hope you'll be able to take off from work, is about fine-tuning. Hopefully, at this point you'll be pretty good at taking tests. If you have seven days off before the exam, continue to take tests but probably not a full one every day. I'd save two or three full exams to take this week and stagger them throughout the week. On the other days, you should go back to problems that you've had trouble with and work on as many of them as you can. The more you see a specific type of problem, the better you'll get at tackling it.

Also, I'd recommend skimming through the *SchweserNotes*™ again this week and going through the *Secret Sauce*®. (I would generally carry the *Secret Sauce*® with me wherever I went during the last two months of studying as it's a great resource and nicely summarizes the material.) I would also use the *Schweser QuikSheet*™, which is three full laminated pages (front and back) of everything you need to know for the level that you are taking. I'd read this on the subway or before bed at night, hoping that it might help the material to sink in. This is a great tool particularly when it comes to some of the material that can be memorized.

Speaking of sleep, you'll also want to get yourself on a regular sleep schedule in the week leading up to the exam, and if you're continuing to do tests, try to do them in the same timeframe that the actual test will be, 9 a.m.—12 noon and then 2 p.m.—5 p.m. Help your body clock get on the schedule it needs to be on for the exam.

On the last day, I'd recommend a combination of final review, rest, and exercise. Don't sit around all day and stare at the *Secret Sauce®*. It'll be the longest day of your life if you do. Trust me, I've done it. Skim through some of the material. Work on final memorization of anything that needs to be memorized, and maybe do just a few problems to give your brain some exercise. But don't overdo it. You want to be fresh going into the exam the next day. If you were a football player preparing for a huge game, you wouldn't completely exert yourself the day before. You'd get some exercise and some rest and try to relax.

Exam Day

Oh, exam day. You are the best and worst of the CFA Program. By the time that first Saturday in June came around every year, it was almost a relief. Sure, you have to go sit in a room all day with complete strangers who secretly wish failure upon you, but hey, after that it's over. It's summer! It's "I don't have to think about this stuff for a long, long time!" But then there's that slightly annoying part of the day that involves actually taking the exam.

So how do you survive exam day? Level 1 comes around twice a year, which gives you a bit of a cushion to screw up, but Levels 2 and 3 come around only once a year. So if you screw it up, like I have three times, you are going to regret it for at least a year and maybe for a lifetime.

INSOMNIA

Now the study guides always tell you to get a good night's sleep, right? Let's start there. One slight problem for me: I was way too nervous to sleep. Call me crazy, but I was completely and utterly aware that I had just wasted six good months of my life studying for what would come down to just one day. My brain would race out of control thinking about how important this day was and how I couldn't screw up. This would generally start about a week before the exam.

So how did I cope? Sleeping pills. Yep, good ol' Ambien. Now look, I don't want to be accused of being or inspiring the Lance Armstrong of financial exams, but the reality is that you need to sleep. In the weeks leading up to the exam, whatever you can do to sleep well, like exercise and eating a healthy diet, is hugely important. But let's be honest, it's really hard to go exercise when you feel like you should be studying. As for eating a healthy diet? Super-important. Did I do it? I was chowing chocolate chips by the handful when studying for these exams. That's healthy, right? I don't know what it was, but I loved chocolate chips when studying.

Anyhow, if you're like me, and your brain gets too worked up to sleep, see if you can get your hands on some sleeping pills. I went to my doctor and just said, "Hey, I'm taking this huge test and I'm too nervous to sleep." He gave me ten pills, which was plenty to a) test them out (word to the wise: don't try a new medicine for the first time the night before the exam), and b) use them when I needed them in the week leading up to test.

If you are suffering from any medical problems while studying for this exam, whether it's sleeplessness, aches and pains, a lack of focus, or even if you think you are prone to panic attacks, it's in your best interest to get in touch with a medical professional. Don't try to self-diagnose. Talk to your doctor. You may be thankful that you did.

PARADISE CITY

Now that we've figured out sleeping, let's talk about location. Where are you going to take the exam? I took Level 1 in NYC, Level 2 in Providence and then in Boston, and Level 3 in Boston twice and Providence once.

Of those three locations, NYC is the biggest. When I took the exam there, we were herded into this massive convention center where you sat in a room with thousands of people. These places tend to be cold and have a very industrial feel to them. The ceilings are a mile high, and in the ultimate "you are being led to the slaughter" move, they lower down a huge metal garage door ten minutes before the start of the exam. This is meant to say to the exam takers either 1) good luck! or 2) you really want to be locked into a warehouse with thousands of other people for an entire day? You got it!

Needless to say, I wasn't a huge fan of the convention center model. Boston and NYC were pretty similar in this regard, although my last time taking an exam in Boston they moved some of us to a hotel ballroom, which was dark, a little bit musty, and overall not much better. The main issue I have with these places is that it's tough to have a pleasant or even civil experience when there are just so many people there. When you have that many people in a room, someone is ALWAYS coughing, sneezing, having some sort of issue that requires a proctor coming over, or any number of other annoyances.

The other thing, of course, is that all of the public facilities are completely overrun. The bathrooms are out of control. (My tip here is to scope them out early and find one that is as far away from the action as possible. People are lazy, and you could probably use the walk.) And of course, the parking lot is usually a mess, and in NYC, good luck trying to get a cab after the test. Believe me, the last thing you want to deal with after this brutal experience is a) trying unsuccessfully for an hour to hail a cab, or b) getting stuck in a traffic jam trying to escape at the same time as thousands of other candidates. I've unfortunately done both.

So what's a good way to do it? How about trying a smaller city? CFA exams are held in cities all over the world. Places like Providence, Rhode Island, have FAR fewer candidates taking exams than the likes of Boston or NYC. I would imagine this is similar outside of the US as well. After taking exams in the big cities, I found Providence to be downright enjoyable. Ok, ok, maybe that's an overstatement, but the logistics were much easier. Providence, for instance, holds the exam at a local community college. There are several classrooms devoted to each level. Taking a test in a classroom, versus a warehouse or ballroom, will definitely feel like a more familiar test-taking setting for you.

Are there downsides to taking the exam in a small city? Sure. The first would be traveling to one if you don't live there. The two times I traveled to Providence (once from NYC and once from Boston), I arrived the afternoon beforehand, got dinner, checked into a local hotel, and tried to get to bed early. Now the potential downside here is obviously that you're not in your own bed and you never know what you're going to get at a hotel. The first time I did this it was fine.

The second time, I wasn't as lucky. I arrived at the hotel where I had booked a room. You can imagine how excited I was to see that multiple high schools were hosting their proms at this venue the same evening, along with several weddings. Great. I needed a good night's sleep and the place was rockin'! I was about to make my third attempt at Level 3. I took my Ambien at about 9 p.m. and basically went right to sleep. The only problem? At 1 a.m. I woke up. I was completely awake with my brain going a mile a minute. It didn't help to wake up to loud music playing, people screaming, and a distinct marijuana odor wafting through my room. Not exactly what I had in mind. I made a spur-of-the-moment decision to take another half of an Ambien, which pretty much knocked me out. I woke the next day feeling pretty groggy, but I rallied in time for the exam.

So think about where you want to take the exam. If you live in NYC or London or some other major city, don't just automatically sign up to take it there. Do you have family close to another test center? Would Mom's home cooking and sleeping in your old room help you, or would your parents just stress you out? Despite my unpleasant hotel experience in Providence, the small-city route worked for me. Taking the test in a big city can be intimidating, ridiculously busy, noisy, and generally distracting.

DON'T BE AN IDIOT

One last but crucial tip about exam day: Don't be an idiot. And I mean that in the most respectful way possible. People study for this exam for six months of their lives. They tell their friends and family they can't see them for half a year. They miss a hundred amazing experiences to do it. Then on exam day, they show up late! Or worse, they show up to the WRONG PLACE. I am absolutely one hundred percent not bullsh*tting you about this. This is way more common than you'd think.

The CFA Institute gives you plenty of information way in advance about 1) where your test is, 2) what you can and can't bring in with you, 3) what type of ID you need, etc. Do yourself a huge favor and look at this stuff. Don't show up with an expired or inappropriate passport or other form of ID and then verbally abuse a proctor for not letting you in. It's not their fault—it's yours. And guess what? They really don't care about how much you studied. They are not CFA charterholders. With all due respect, I'm quite sure they have no clue how big of a deal this test is. They care about their eight-hour workday, not the three hundred hours you put into preparing!

Here's what I did to take the stress out of this aspect of exam day: I showed up with my exam ticket and an acceptable (non-expired!) form of ID. I knew that my calculator was one of the approved models and I had extra batteries for it. I had my earplugs and my pens and pencils, and I always showed up about an hour and fifteen minutes before the exam. It sounds corny, but I'd recommend doing a practice run to the exam site. Go on a Saturday morning a week or two before the exam at the same time you'd need to go for the real thing. Make sure you know how to drive there, walk there, subway there, or whatever you're planning to do. Time your trip, and factor in variables like traffic, subway delays, and so forth. Then on exam day, build in an extra fifteen minutes just for added safety. I can't tell you how many people show up late to these tests. It's ridiculous!

Of course, if you're not there on time, they lock you out. They typically shut the doors thirty minutes before the start of the exam. Those who were there on time get to spend what is one of the most tense, nerve-racking half hours of their lives sitting quietly and twiddling their thumbs while exam booklets are passed out, instructions are read, and ultimately the test begins. But they've got it good! The poor souls who were late spend what is most likely one of the most anger-filled half hours of their lives standing outside the doors waiting to be let in. Only several minutes after the exam commences do they let these stragglers in. These folks then must not only go through the process of filling out their name, candidate number, etc., but they then have the unenviable task of making up ten or fifteen minutes on the competition, who they are of course being graded against on a curve.

Do yourself a favor. Get your act together. Check your ID, exam ticket, and test location. Plan out your route and leave yourself enough time to get there. What the CFA Institute decides to put on the exam is out of your hands, but these are things *you* can control. Do it.

IRRATIONAL EXUBERANCE

If we assume that you eventually found your way to the exam site and took the test, well then, after about eight or nine hours on the scene, you're going to be looking forward to busting out of those doors a little bit after 5 p.m. Studying for the CFA is a long drawn-out process, and it's only natural to want to blow off a little steam after the big test. But if you plan to make booze part of your post-exam festivities, let me just advise you from personal experience— BE CAREFUL!

I basically stopped alcohol consumption for the last few months of studying every year. Not that I can really consume much these days anyhow; somewhere along the line any more than three drinks became an automatic hangover, which certainly didn't mix well with attempting to study. I advise you to be careful when partying post-exam because if you are like me, your body will not be used to excess. Believe me, some of the worst hangovers in my life came the morning after CFA exams. And I can tell you from personal experience that battling a brutal hangover is absolutely not the best way to spend your first day of freedom after six long months of studying. You have been warned!

ONE DOWN, TWO TO GO

So let's assume that you are able to clear all of these hurdles. You organize a weekly calendar that spans six months and you stick to it. You put in your 250-300 hours of study time. You take plenty of practice tests. You get a good night's sleep before the exam. You show up to the *right* exam location with the correct form of identification. And maybe, just maybe, you heed my advice on not going overboard in your post-exam celebrations . . .

Well then, congratulations! You've put in a heck of an effort and you should be commended. You'll have to hold out eight weeks for your results, but if you've done everything we've talked about, I think there is a darn good chance that you'll pass this exam.

If you do indeed pass Level 1, the trap that you'll most want to avoid falling into is developing a false sense of confidence. You may pass this exam and think 1) I'm awesome! How many people can I tell about this? 2) That was kind of hard, but I'm super-smart so Level 2 will be a breeze, and 3) Time to sign up for Level 2 and figure out my timeline so I can study exactly the same way for the second one as I did the first. And on all three counts, you would be mistaken. Or, at least I was.

If you happen to fail, the most likely reason is that you did not put in the appropriate amount of study time. It's time to regroup and reconsider how committed you are to this goal. If you want it badly enough, then it's time to get back on the horse and start planning your next attempt. With the right plan and the right level of commitment, Level 1 is an exam you can absolutely pass.

For those experiencing the sugar high of passing, congratulations again! Your reward? The right to take an even harder test!

Chapter 5 Checklist:	
☑ **Do:**	☒ **Don't:**
☑ 1) Map out a week-by-week calendar of your study plan and stick to it!	☒ 1) Think that you can get by with an ad-hoc plan.
☑ 2) Consider what test location might provide you with the best exam experience.	☒ 2) Automatically sign up for the nearest test location without considering the pros and cons.
☑ 3) Make at least one "test run" to your exam location and double-check your logistics.	☒ 3) Show up late or without the proper identification on exam day.
☑ 4) Celebrate responsibly.	☒ 4) Overindulge after the exam.

CHAPTER 6:

Level 2

* Moving On Up
* What's It All About?
* Known Unknowns
* Fight for Your Right to Third Party
* Take Tests, Take Tests, Take Tests
* Now, Take More Tests
* The Sour Taste of Failure
* Team Player
* Do Pass Go, Do Collect $200

MOVING ON UP

I took Level 1 in December 2007, so I rolled right into Level 2 in June of 2008. No problem, right? Might as well start studying again while all this stuff is fresh in my head, you know? Well . . . turns out it wasn't that simple.

The reality, as I soon would discover, is that Level 2 is an absolute beast. Not only does the curriculum cover an almost unbelievably broad scope, but unlike Level 1, there is a huge focus here on calculations and working out sometimes very long and always extremely difficult problems.

Additionally, while there may be a small amount of material that you'll see again from Level 1, it's probably not accurate to say that Level 2 "builds on" Level 1. Each level, in my experience, is a completely different animal unto itself. In retrospect, I came into Level 2 not giving the test enough respect. And quite frankly, I couldn't afford to do that, because it would be the hardest test that I had ever taken in my life (up to that point).

WHAT'S IT ALL ABOUT?

As for the material itself, as you probably know, Level 2 is much more "calculation intensive" than Level 1, and than Level 3 for that matter.

The way I studied for Level 2 the first time was all wrong and ultimately, I believe, the reason why I failed. I approached it like every other test I'd ever taken and tried to memorize things. Like I did with Level 1, I literally re-wrote the *SchweserNotes*™ in my notebooks multiple times. In the past, this tactic had resulted in the information slowly being absorbed into my brain. I think it's called osmosis.

But this didn't work for Level 2. The problem was that the Level 2 material was much more complicated. The concepts are much more developed than in Level 1, and the detail with which you need to know them in order to perform calculations is incredible.

I started using some other Schweser tools at this stage as well, videos and flash cards and the like. There were some helpful things about the videos; I enjoyed hearing people talk about the concepts, etc., but ultimately I don't think viewing these lectures was the most effective use of my time. I would have been wise to use this time taking tests.

KNOWN UNKNOWNS

My problem with the heavy focus on calculations in Level 2 (and this plagued me on Level 3 as well) is that I knew the concepts but would inevitably make a math error, which would screw up my answers. You'd think you might be ok on a multiple-choice exam, but conveniently the CFA Institute would make that same math error then put that *wrong* answer on the multiple choice as well. Pretty sneaky, right? Well, it certainly seems that way when you are going through the process. You think, "How could these guys be so heartless as to do the entire calculation and then make a stupid error right at the end and then put THAT wrong answer as a choice?"

I'll admit that it does seem pretty heartless, and I hated the test writers for a while. But then of course you realize that they *have* to do that. Really smart, really driven people study for these tests. How do you differentiate between them? They need to have some way to do it. Someone needs to pass and someone needs to fail. Rightly or wrongly, often the best way they can make that differentiation is by purposefully making a stupid mistake that they know a lot of people will make, and then putting that as an answer.

I fell into these traps more times than I'd care to admit. But eventually I learned to avoid the land mines. Many times, if you get to the end of doing a major calculation and your answer matches up with theirs, you are wrong. How could this be? It's multiple choice, right? Their answer matches my answer. I'm good to go, right? Nope.

As I've mentioned, I failed Level 2 the first time I took it. I pinned this on three reasons: 1) not having enough time after taking Level 1 in December to truly grasp the Level 2 material by June, 2) not being a math person, and 3) trying to plan a wedding (or at least the band!) at the same time.

The reality is that I didn't know how to study for such a test. Beyond that—and it sounds funny to say—but I didn't know how well I actually needed to know the concepts. Donald Rumsfeld is famous for his "known unknowns" phrase. In my case, I knew what I needed to know, but I didn't know how well I needed to know it. Confused yet? I certainly was.

FIGHT FOR YOUR RIGHT TO THIRD PARTY

So what *did* help me? Third-party study notes were probably the tool that helped me most throughout the CFA exam process. One of the big questions people struggle with is whether or not the third-party study notes are sufficient to rely on to pass the exams.

In general, third-party notes do an excellent job of covering the material that you need to know for each level. I wouldn't waste too much time looking at those "refresher" books for previous levels, as what you need to know for Level 2 is in the Level 2 curriculum, and therefore the study notes. There's a very, very, very slim chance that you encounter something on a test that was from a previous level and not mentioned in the curriculum for the level that you are on. But that chance is so slim that I really would not worry about it.

Almost everything that can be tested in any given level will be in the third-party study notes for *that* level. I say *almost* everything because there are things that come up on the test, again *very* rarely, that weren't in the notes. Generally speaking, though, I found the *SchweserNotes*™ to be comprehensive and well put together, and I would absolutely recommend them to anyone and everyone. Frankly, I couldn't have passed a single level without them.

There are other providers out there as well. 7city® and Stalla® come to mind. I know that 7city® often combines their program with in-person learning opportunities: classes, seminars, etc., as do some of the other providers. Stalla®, along with some other providers, I know less about, but I'd take some time to look into what each provider offers and, as previously discussed, whether your employer might have a deal with any of them.

I became very comfortable with Schweser and thought of them (rightly or wrongly) as the go-to provider for CFA-related resources, but many other people have had success with other providers. This is a personal decision. Some of it will stem from what is available to you (i.e., does your employer pay for one particular provider?) and/or what is convenient for you (i.e., does 7city® offer a weekly class in your neighborhood?), etc.

I self-studied from the *SchweserNotes*™. As I've mentioned, I also tried out the Schweser video instruction. What they do for the videos is provide you with a couple of books that are chock full of PowerPoint-like slides that cover the entire curriculum. Then, you can either watch a recorded session (online or DVD) with a professor who talks you through the material and then talks through some problems, *or* you can join the class online in real time, which allows you to submit questions. I used these types of videos twice (for my second attempt at Level 2 and first attempt at Level 3).

Then of course there are actual live (in-person) classes and seminars. I mentioned that I signed up for a CFA class back in the early 2000s where just one night in attendance was enough to scare me off for a few years. I also signed up for one of Schweser's three-day seminars on my second attempt at Level 3. I only attended Day 1 until the lunch break.

I don't have anything particularly bad to say about these live seminars or classes. In fact, many people like that these classes "force" them to be on a specific study schedule. But they weren't the right learning environment for me, personally. I discovered that I learned best at home from a book. Or, in reality, by taking tests.

My thinking, especially for the three-day seminar, went something like this: "I've committed to using these three days to study for the CFA exam. Is my time really best spent sitting in this hotel ballroom listening to a professor I can hardly hear where I may or may not garner a useful tidbit of information or two, or . . . should I be at home hammering practice tests?"

The choice was obvious to me. But again, a completely personal decision. Some people rave about live classes and seminars. It gives them a chance to interact with other candidates and, perhaps more importantly, to ask questions to a professor who knows the material well. It depends on your learning style.

TAKE TESTS, TAKE TESTS, TAKE TESTS

One thing, in my opinion, that is consistent no matter what your learning style might be, is the importance of practice exams. When I started studying for Level 2, I was under the impression that learning the concepts and doing a few tests would get me by. I was wrong. It turns out that you *really* need to learn the concepts—inside and out. The CFA Institute will think of every possible way to twist and turn the material to the point that you will be staring at a question on the exam and thinking to yourself: "I don't even know how to approach this. I just studied for six months nonstop and I don't even know what these guys are *asking* for." Believe me, it will happen. I distinctly remember feeling this way on multiple occasions.

The only, and I mean the only, way to properly prepare yourself for this is by taking tests. There is something about the way you learn the material that can only be garnered from taking tests. Memorizing won't do it. Reading won't do it. Listening to a professor talk won't do it. Taking tests hammers the concepts into your head, and that is what you need.

NOW, TAKE MORE TESTS

You MUST get your hands on every past exam you can. Take all of the Schweser exams, mock exams, and any other exam you can find (Boston Security Analysts Society, current year and past years, etc.) For the BSAS exam, you need to pay a fee to get the exam from them, but it's probably worth it as they usually create a very high-quality exam. Otherwise, as we've already discussed, you need to work your network and do as much online investigation as you can to track down relevant practice exams.

The one thing I didn't grasp until my final exam—my sixth attempt—was how important practice exams were. Crazy that it took me that long, right? Well, I hope reading this book will help you to figure that out *much* sooner.

THE SOUR TASTE OF FAILURE

Failure. It's really not an easy thing to deal with. And Level 2 gave me my first taste of CFA failure. If you want to put a silver lining on a dark cloud, it's that studying for a test the second time around gets easier. I noticed this the second time I took Levels 2 and 3. The extra utility from studying the same material a *third* time is not nearly as incremental in my opinion, but hopefully you'll never be in a position to opine on that topic. I only had to do it once, and I can tell you that by the time you are studying for an exam the third time, you are on a completely different level. More on that later.

But studying something a second time around *is* helpful. I remember learning the Level 2 and Level 3 curriculums on a much deeper level the second time I studied each of them. Of course, there is a concern that you may gloss over some concepts that you think you know, which is a fair concern, but one which I think is outweighed by the ability to get a much better understanding of the concepts that you clearly didn't master the first time around.

Failing Level 2 was difficult to accept, but I did feel like I failed when I walked out of the exam. You always hope for the best, but it was pretty clear to me that I had studied the wrong way.

Not to sound pompous, but failing was not something I was particularly used to in most aspects of my life. Like many kids, I was lucky enough to be told that I was special, smart, and talented growing up. I was also one of those kids who did pretty well in school.

The reason I mention this is that many people who take the CFA have never really been knocked down before academically. They have been overachievers their entire lives. The CFA is really the first time where they have a very real chance of encountering failure. I mean the chances of passing all three exams their first time around is less than one in ten, and we're not talking about competing against the general population here. We are talking about competing against people who, in all likelihood, have already cleared many impressive hurdles in their lives including graduating from prestigious universities or landing jobs with top investment firms. In other words, the competition is pretty stiff.

Of course, no one is likely to shed a tear for overachievers failing at something in life, especially overachievers on Wall Street. Cry me a river, right? I didn't go looking for sympathy either when I failed. In fact, when I failed Level 2, it wasn't such a shock to me.

But to many overachievers that first failure really is a shock. Then there is a bit of self-pity and self-blame. As in, "Obviously, I'm smart enough to pass this test. I can't believe I didn't study harder." Then of course there is embarrassment: "What will my friends think? My colleagues at work? My parents? My parents have never seen me fail at anything!" My only advice here would be to look at the numbers. With pass rates so shockingly low, the reality is that even if you've been an overachiever your entire life, as most CFA candidates have been, you are likely to fail (at least one) of these tests. I know that's not exactly a pep talk. But it's the truth.

TEAM PLAYER

In a way, I kind of like the idea of overachievers failing. It fosters humility. The CFA exams taught me a lot about humility and a lot about empathy. Somewhere along the path to your CFA charter, you stop rooting for other people to fail and start rooting for them to pass. Don't get me wrong, I know this thing is on a curve and I wasn't rooting for a hundred-percent pass rate. I'm talking about rooting for people you know, who have worked hard and deserve success.

When I took Level 1, I thought, "Well, it'll stink if I fail, but God help me, *that* guy better not freakin' pass or I'll kill myself!" But by the time I was deep into Level 3, several failures later, it was no longer me against the world. It was me against me. Was I determined enough? Was I disciplined enough? That could only be determined between me, myself, and I.

The CFA exam process is a personal, private experience in many ways, but don't discount the fact that being a "team player," in a sense, has its benefits. As you move through the CFA levels, your peers, colleagues, and fellow test-takers will often be in the same boat. It's much more rewarding to empathize with these people, to help them, and to feel their pain or elation as they go through this process than it is too root against them. I mean, who wants to be miserable when someone else achieves something great? That attitude stinks. The CFA exams helped to teach me this lesson and I'm better for it. I hope you will be, too.

DO PASS GO, DO COLLECT $200

Passing, that's a pretty cool thing to do. The second time I took Level 2, I knew I had hit the tests much harder and came away feeling an incredible sense of accomplishment walking out of the exam room. I knew I had passed and it felt great. When you pass Level 2, you also pass the theoretical point of no return when it comes to the CFA. Lots of people take and even pass Level 1, but Level 2? That's a whole different ballgame. If you pass Level 2, you've passed a *major* weeding-out stage.

Level 2 is a serious exam. There is really no other way to put it. You have to master the ins and outs of some incredibly difficult subjects. If you've made it to this point, you should feel pretty good about yourself. As I mentioned, many see this point as the point of no return. That's a good thing, right? Well . . . it depends.

When I passed Level 2, I thought for the first time, "Wow, I am really going to do this. I am *actually* going to be a CFA charterholder." I had fantasized about having those three letters in the past, but I hadn't actually been confident that I would do it. If I'd failed Level 2 again, I'm pretty sure I would have packed it in and lived out the rest of my life as someone who passed Level 1 of the CFA. Not bad, but not exactly awe-inspiring either.

When you pass Level 2, you feel like you are ready to conquer the world, because there is just one level between you and those three letters. Just one measly level! And it's Level 3, for crying out loud! I mean, isn't that the level where half of the answers are written? Written! That's right, we're talking open-ended answers. Please, how hard could it possibly be?

So I moved on to Level 3 with complete determination. I told everyone who would listen that for me, Level 3 was a "one and done" deal. That's right. Sorry friends. Sorry family. You're not going to see me for six months. I am ordering those books as soon as I can and cracking them in December . . . no . . . November! My plan was to disappear off the face of the earth for six months and emerge in June damn confident of passing that exam.

But as we know, things don't always work out the way we plan them . . .

Chapter 6 Checklist:	
☑ **Do:**	☒ **Don't:**
☑ 1) Realize that the Level 2 exam will probably be the hardest test you have ever taken in your life.	☒ 1) Take it lightly and assume you can study for it like any other test.
☑ 2) Take TONS of practice exams.	☒ 2) Rely on reading the material numerous times or watching online video instruction.
☑ 3) Concentrate on becoming an expert at actually taking exams.	☒ 3) Assume that if you know the material well, you will pass.
☑ 4) Figure out how you learn best (classroom, self-study, etc.) and spend the majority of your time studying that way.	☒ 4) Waste precious time using study methods that don't work for you.
☑ 5) Root for your fellow test-takers, especially the ones you know.	☒ 5) Root against other test-takers.

CHAPTER 7:

Level 3

* The Final Countdown
* Write for Your Life
* A Survival Game
* Moment of Truth
* School's Out
* Knocked Down, But Not Out
* Back in the Ring
* Ripping My Heart Out, Along the Perforated Line
* I Ain't Goin' Out Like That
* Sorry, Suckers . . .

THE FINAL COUNTDOWN

Ah, Level 3. You almost defeated me. But I won the war. Let me just state the obvious: it's really hard to study your tail off for six months only to fail an exam. It's even harder to pick yourself up, dust yourself off, and give it another go. Doing it a third time? That is where you encounter the not-so-well-defined territory at the intersection of insane stubbornness, unrealistic optimism, stupidity, and despair. For me, Level 3 was the most visceral experience of my life. I have never failed yet ultimately succeeded so fantastically in my life.

I underestimated Level 3. I was determined to take and pass this test *the first time*. I told my wife and anyone who would listen that I was going to study my butt off for this exam and take it once. That's it. So I set out to study as much as humanly possible, and that's what I did. I absolutely put in the hours. In fact, I'm pretty sure I put in north of three hundred hours this time around. But ultimately, I studied the wrong way. By this time, I was beyond trying to re-write entire volumes of *SchweserNotes*™ in my notebooks, but I still wasn't using my time wisely.

Sure, just like I did for every level, I dedicated every weekend from December to June to studying. But again, I failed to take enough tests. Instead I spent my time reading the material over and over again. Given the focus in Level 3 on Behavioral Finance and GIPS®, two of the more qualitative topic areas in the entire three-level curriculum, I thought I could again memorize my way through as I'd done with Level 1. I spent hours and hours trying to make sure I knew every term and every GIPS® rule. Of course, you do need to know all that stuff, but just as importantly, you need to see over and over again how this material is going to be twisted and turned into an exam-style format to really get a grasp of how the test writers are going to try to trip you up. Simply knowing definitions is not enough to get by.

Again, I spent too many hours viewing video instruction. Some people may learn effectively this way so I don't want to discount it, but in retrospect it was not a good use of my time. It's actually kind of nice to sit back, watch a video of a professor explaining a concept, and follow along on your slides, but this was not enough to pound the concepts into my head. Everyone learns differently to some extent, and though it took me longer than it should have to figure it out, I know now that I learn by doing. I learn by taking exams. Lots and lots and lots of exams.

WRITE FOR YOUR LIFE

The most frustrating thing about Level 3 in my opinion is that it seemed awfully arbitrary. The morning session of the Level 3 exam consists of so-called "constructed response" questions. Most candidates refer to this as the "essay" section, but that's probably a bit of a stretch as they are not asking you to write a book. You are writing a few sentences in response to a given question or even structuring your answer in bullet points, which is a perfectly acceptable format. The point is that you are not choosing from A, B, or C but rather providing your own answer. Going into Level 3, I had thought that such a format would be an absolute strength for me, but in reality, it turned into an absolute nightmare. Time and time again, when I took practice tests or even filled in the Schweser End of Chapter questions that dealt with setting up an "Investment Policy Statement," I found that my answers didn't match up with their answers. My answers, I thought, were perfectly logical, but then again, so were theirs. It wasn't black and white, and by this stage my brain had been trained to look for the "right" answer, so I found this incredibly frustrating.

The questions would ask you to make qualitative judgment calls on whether an imaginary investor should be considered more or less risk-averse based on a whole load of factors, and the way that I viewed them was often different from the way the test writer viewed them. It all seemed so incredibly arbitrary to me, and it was this element of the Level 3 exam that was harder to study for than any other part of the CFA exams.

I'd expected to nail the essays on Level 3, but when it came down to it, I longed for the straightforwardness of having to pick A, B, or C. At least in that case when you got an answer wrong on a practice test, you could go back and figure out why and then correct it the next time through. But with the Level 3 essays, I'd read the provided answer and my answer and think, "My answer is better and makes more sense." But unfortunately there's no taking the CFA grader out for a beer to argue about it. You're either right or wrong, so you need to figure out what *they* think is right and make sure you put that down as your answer.

As a quick aside if you *wanted* to try to take your CFA grader out for a beer . . .

I often wondered what would happen if I showed up to "CFA Mecca" aka Charlottesville, Virginia, during the grading process and tried to track down the poor soul trying to make sense of my Level 3 essay responses.

Apparently, the grading of these exams is quite the event. Not much is officially made public about the process, but if you believe CFA lore, it's essentially a two-week-long party where "the chosen" charterholders, typically the same group every year (or close to it), descend upon Charlottesville to grade tests by day and drink wine and get down to country music by night. You can imagine running into this crowd at one of the local watering holes. While I'm sure they are all lovely people (and brilliant too!), they'd just have to be the nerdiest group of people you'd ever set eyes on, wouldn't they? Well, I don't know, Star Trek convention-goers might have something to say about that.

Anyhow, the closest you can get to "schmoozing" your test-grader is paying the hundred-dollar fee to have your test "retabulated." I, of course, have done that. It's probably not worth it as I think they basically just make sure you didn't write your answers on a page that they didn't see before (i.e., they are not actually re-reading and re-grading the whole thing), but after you've already spent so much time and money trying to pass the test, what's another hundred bucks, right? Sigh.

A SURVIVAL GAME

The best way to get a sense for what the graders want is to take past years' tests and compare your answers with the answers provided. The CFA Institute makes several years of morning sessions available to you each year, and if you're smart, you can usually find even more exams from other sources. As I've already noted, I tend to place more value on tests that were written by the CFA Institute, because even if the curriculum changes a bit from year to year, it's important to have a really good feel for how they ask questions and what they expect answer-wise.

The good news about the essay questions is that generally everyone does pretty poorly on them. No one writes exactly what the test writers were looking for. People interpret things differently and come up with different ways of answering the questions. The key is to set up your answers in such a way that you give the grader as much opportunity as possible to give you points. As you take more and more practice exams, you'll learn that things like using bullet points and key terms or buzzwords all increase your chances of getting points. After all, the morning session of Level 3 is a *survival* game. You need to write enough relevant things in enough of a coherent manner to stay in the game. Then you can move on to the afternoon section and really slay the multiple choice. Who would have thought three hours of multiple choice could ever feel so refreshing?

MOMENT OF TRUTH

When that first weekend in June rolled around and it was time for me to take my first crack at Level 3, I felt like I was in a pretty good position to nail the exam. Thinking back, I was definitely lulled into a false sense of security because Level 3 was so qualitative. I mean, Ethics, Behavioral Finance, and GIPS®? Time to go ahead and order those new business cards, right? Since it's quite difficult to self-grade your own essay responses on practice exams, I don't think I even realized how poorly prepared I was for the morning session.

In fact, I felt quite confident even after completing my exam on that warm Saturday afternoon in June. I walked out and thought, "Yep, I just passed that sucker." But of course what I told people was, "Oh, you never know."

No one ever means what they say when coming out of the CFA exams. They need to walk the tightrope of managing expectations with their family, friends, and colleagues. When someone asks, "How did you do?" they may be tempted to lie, exaggerate, broadcast their incompetence, or be humble. I composed this table to help you translate what a CFA candidate thinks about their prospects for passing the exam.

"How did you do on the test?"	
What they say:	**What they mean:**
I nailed it.	I'm a jerk and/or I'm incompetent.
Not sure, it was hard.	I may have gotten every answer right.
Failed it.	Passed it.
Absolute utter disaster, no chance.	Probably failed it but still hopeful.

SCHOOL'S OUT

Either way, when you walk out of the exam, especially if you think you've done well, there is a certain "last day of school" feeling. I think I sang the lyrics to Alice Cooper's "School's Out" as I walked out of every test. You know it . . . "Schoooool's out for SUMMER. Schoooool's out forEVER!" It's a great feeling.

And for better or for worse, it takes the CFA Institute a heck of a long time to get the results back to you, so you don't have to think about anything CFA-related for a long while. After thinking of nothing *but* the CFA exam for six months, this is actually quite a relief.

For Levels 1 and 2, according to the CFA Institute website, it takes them eight weeks to get the results back to you. So with the test always on the first Saturday in June, that generally puts you right at the end of July. Most people are surprised that it takes so long for the first two levels since they are completely multiple choice. Apparently, though, it's not as simple as just running the Scantron answer sheets through a grading machine and sending them on their way. There are questions that candidates complain about or think were unfair. There are questions that people will claim had multiple acceptable answers. So the CFA Institute needs to sort through those issues. And, then of course they need to decide what the passing grade or "minimum passing score" will be. This is an interesting dynamic because they do not tell you what grade you need to pass ahead of time. It is determined subsequently as candidates are essentially graded on a curve. Conventional wisdom says that seventy is a good estimate for the percentage of questions you need to answer correctly. That's only a C- in school, right? Shouldn't be too difficult. Except of course, it is.

For Level 3, it takes approximately ten weeks for the results to come out, which puts you somewhere in mid-August. The good news is that they'll tell you in advance the exact day that you can expect your results, although by this time, your CFA experience that first weekend in June is but a distant memory. The incremental time for the grading of Level 3 presumably allows them a couple of extra weeks to decipher the chicken scratch that makes up most people's essay responses.

KNOCKED DOWN, BUT NOT OUT

So I had that August day circled on my calendar and it finally arrived. Yes, this was the fateful day when I'd hear the long-awaited and hopefully triumphant news of my Level 3 labor of love. The news that I was done with the CFA Program forever! My parents, my wife's parents, and my wife and I were all staying at a bed and breakfast in Cape Cod for the weekend. What a great time to find out that I passed Level 3. It would be a weekend of celebration. We would eat and drink and talk about how I, Greg Campion, would soon be "Greg Campion, CFA."

I woke up that rainy August morning and realized I had left my Blackberry in my car. Everyone knew I was getting my results. I ran out to get my Blackberry with my wife at my side. "Here goes nothing," I said. I opened up the email and there it was. FAIL.

I'll give the CFA Institute some credit. They don't beat around the bush when they tell you your results. When you fail, you fail. You see the word FAIL in big, bold letters in the opening paragraph of their email.

It is a sinking, soul-destroying punch to the gut.

Believe it or not, it is still painful now to write about that moment. I was crushed. Absolutely crushed. I was so sure I had passed that exam. In fact, I had come as close to passing as you can without . . . well . . . passing. The CFA Institute divides the failed candidates into bands 1 through 10. If you were in band 10, you were in the top ten percent of failed candidates. That's where I was. Band 10. I don't know if it makes it better or worse to find out how close you were to passing in the presence of that awful word: FAIL. Maybe it doesn't matter. Failing is failing.

I would either have to quit, which would mean that I was indeed a failure, or do the whole thing over. I knew what that meant in terms of time and effort. Heartbreaking.

As with most things in life, the people around you take your failure much worse than you do. Despite the fact that I was heartbroken, I accepted the result pretty quickly. I sulked for a few minutes with my wife. She said how sorry she was for me, and she really was.

My parents came down for breakfast soon after and asked me right away about the results. They were devastated. My mom cried. They felt so bad for me and just couldn't get over it. They cared about me. A parent wants their child to succeed. I think back now and I am thankful for how hard my parents took the news. Without getting too sappy, it's tough times like these that show you how much the people in your life care about you. It also shows you what you are made of.

BACK IN THE RING

I decided to take Level 3 again. How could I quit after coming so far? Of course the CFA curriculum teaches you about sunk costs. What's gone is gone, right? All the time, the effort, and money that I had put into the previous exams . . . those were just sunk costs.

But I decided to stay the course. I would full-on study for the exam again. I'd start in December and I'd study my butt off again for six months. I would continue to miss out on life for another year. Weddings, parties, family gatherings—you name it. I was signing up for another year of missing my life.

Only this time, the stakes were higher. Whitney and I found out late that year that she was expecting our first child in July. We were absolutely thrilled and couldn't wait to be parents. This news also meant that it really was my last time taking this test. Whitney was getting pretty fed up with me studying my entire life away, and who could blame her? She wasn't signing up to be a single parent.

The impending birth of my child gave me extra motivation to pass the exam. I actually remember thinking that this was no longer about me, it was about my child. I needed to pass this test for my unborn child. Why? I didn't want to fathom having to miss out on my child's life to study for it a third time. But I also wanted my child to be proud of me. I remember thinking that it would be cool to talk to my children someday about perseverance and how I failed over and over again but ultimately succeeded. I also remember thinking how disappointing it would be to have to explain to my children someday what happened if I failed. To come all that way, to study so many times, to give up so much of my life, and then come up empty-handed? It wasn't the kind of example I wanted to set for my children.

So, I got after it once again. As my wife prepared for our child pretty much singlehandedly, I did what I always did. I studied. She bought the maternity clothes, went to the showers, even set up the entire nursery. I studied. She read *What to Expect When You're Expecting*. I studied.

I hated feeling like I was missing out. Not only did I feel like I was not doing my husbandly duties and being a good partner to my wife, I felt like I was doing an injustice to my unborn child.

That said, in my mind, the ends justified the means. My career prospects would be brighter with a CFA charter, and in fact we started thinking really seriously about moving to the South. We wanted to be closer to my wife's family; to raise our kids near their close-in-age cousins, and basically center our life around our family rather than our jobs. I knew that I would have to quit my job to make the move possible, so having the CFA on my CV would be absolutely huge heading to a part of the country where I knew no one.

I could power through this one more time. I'd go hardcore study mode for six months, and then I was free to be a dad and husband and forget about this bullsh*t forever. So I studied. I studied and studied and studied.

RIPPING MY HEART OUT, ALONG THE PERFORATED LINE

And then came the big day . . . again. Unfortunately, my second attempt at Level 3 turned out to be one of the worst days of my life. I arrived that morning to the dimly lit hotel ballroom, where the exam was taking place, fully planning to pass that test. I chatted with a coworker for a little while as we mulled around the exam room before taking our seats. I also exchanged pleasantries and some gallows humor with a client who was sitting nearby. Joking around on exam days helped to calm my nerves.

And then the test began. Right back into the mix. The morning didn't go well, mysterious essay questions and all, but I felt I could make up for it in the afternoon.

But it was not meant to be. Moments before the afternoon session began, I accidentally ripped out an extra page of my exam book. A proctor appeared, took my maligned exam booklet, and went off to get me another. The only problem was that the exam was starting. Sweating bullets, I waited. Finally, five minutes into the exam, I got my new book.

To say I was flustered would be an understatement as would be the fact that I rushed through the exam in a panicked flurry. Not only was I attempting to pass one of the hardest examinations on earth, but I felt I had nowhere near the amount of time I needed. My panic had spiraled out of control and put me in what was probably one of the worst states of mind that I'd ever experienced. When time was up, and we handed in our test booklets, it was obvious to me that I had just bombed that exam.

As I was leaving the test room, a client I ran into claimed that she thought she'd failed. I believed her. She said she was done for good. My colleague claimed that he failed. I claimed that I failed. We would all turn out to be right.

This was the most devastating failure to date. I didn't have to wait for the results to know that I failed. Sure, I secretly held out hope, but I knew right away that I had failed. I remember leaving the hotel parking garage and there was a huge traffic jam of people trying to get out. I was so depressed. I lay awake that night in bed thinking about how I had just blown two years worth of work. Devastating.

"That was it. I'm done," I told my family, friends, and work colleagues. Many people couldn't believe that I would quit at this stage, but many others were just happy to see me be done with it. Nobody really blamed me for quitting. It was understandable. Even though I had made it so close to the finish line, I had given up too much of my life. I had attempted Level 3 twice and failed twice. The CFA exams would be a footnote on my life, but in the end, I'd have nothing to show for them. It bothered me, but I couldn't fathom another attempt.

My son was born in July of that year. It was one of the happiest events of my life. My wife and I struggled through the sleepless nights in the first few months but ultimately got more and more comfortable with our new roles.

The fall came and went and I felt no desire to take Level 3 for a third time. It did weigh on me that I'd always have this failure on my record, though. I wondered if I should remove all references to the CFA Program from my CV and LinkedIn profile. I felt that there was no way to show I'd succeeded at Levels 1 and 2 without also showing that I was ultimately a failure. I couldn't shake the nagging disappointment.

The winter came and went, and I still did not feel the urge to take the test again. I usually started studying for the exam in December or January, at the latest. In March, it finally hit me: "Am I really done with this thing? Can I really just let this thing be? Am I willing to live with this failure for the rest of my life? Will I regret it? How much will I regret it? I know this material so damn well. Is it a total shame to not take this test again?"

I AIN'T GOIN' OUT LIKE THAT

By sheer stubbornness, or stupidity, or at this stage quite possibly addiction, I signed up for the test again. Yep. One more time.

I did things differently this time around. First of all, I hardly told a soul I was taking it. My immediate family knew, and that's about it. I barely talked about it. I thought they had had enough of hearing about it, and quite frankly I think I had just reached a stage of embarrassment about the whole thing. I wanted to keep a low profile.

I told no one at work. I was even asked point-blank on several occasions if I was taking the exam and said no.

I also, of course, had a baby boy. I was determined not to ignore him. Starting in March meant studying for only three months—half the time I'd taken in the past. Even less than that, really, considering that I decided to only study on weekends (i.e., no weeknights).

My wife was begrudgingly supportive, and once again was the true hero in the process, taking the lead in spending time with our son. Even with a scaled-back study schedule, I missed out on a lot of little trips to the park, but was able to stay more closely connected to my son than I thought would be possible.

I knew the material pretty darn well at this point since I'd studied it completely twice before, so I decided that I'd basically bomb through the Schweser books once quickly and then pretty much just start taking tests.

And that's what I did. I got my hands on every test I could find. In the end, I probably doubled the number of tests I had taken for prior exams. I was definitely well into the double digits in terms of the number of full six-hour exams I took, but I lost count somewhere along the way. Actual CFA exams, mock CFA exams, Schweser exams, BSAS exams, online question banks—you name it, I took it! I took so many exams—I mean SO many exams—that I became an expert in . . . well . . . taking exams.

How had it possibly taken me this long to figure this out? As I took more exams, I got better at them. I started to see where test writers were trying to trip me up in the questions.

SORRY, SUCKERS . . .

I decided to take the exam in Providence. As I mentioned earlier, I had taken one of my Level 2 attempts there and really liked the small classroom feel. I confidently walked in and sat down for the exam. The morning went well. I felt like I knew the material and recognized where they were trying to trip me up. I called my wife at lunch and told her I thought it was going well. She was encouraging as always. The afternoon, too, went well—amazingly well. I felt like I knew absolutely everything on that exam. I was spotting little trick questions left and right, and for some reason every time I found one, I'd think, "Sorry, suckers, but I'm not falling for this."

I walked out of that exam feeling like an absolute rock star. I felt great. I was so glad I didn't give up. I also felt thankful that my wife had put up with me doing these tests for so long, especially the last one, for which she had to singlehandedly chase our little boy around.

I was happy. Fittingly, one of my best friends from high school was having his bachelor party that evening. I drove to pick up a friend who happened to live in Providence and we went to the casinos in Connecticut for a night of partying. I was so grateful to spend time with my friends. I hardly mentioned the fact that I had just sat through a grueling test all day long. I was just happy it was done.

Chapter 7 Checklist:	
☑ **Do:**	☒ **Don't:**
☑ 1) Realize that the qualitative nature of Level 3 provides a whole host of unique challenges.	☒ 1) Assume that Level 3 will be a breeze if you're a good writer.
☑ 2) Spend time learning what test graders are looking for in ideal essay responses.	☒ 2) Assume that if an answer makes sense to you, it will be adequate.
☑ 3) Take tests, take tests, take tests. Now, take more tests.	☒ 3) Try to breeze through without putting in the hard work. This means practice tests.
☑ 4) Use your setbacks and failures as motivation.	☒ 4) Give up.

CHAPTER 8:

Life after the CFA

* Signed, Sealed, Delivered
* Back of the Closet
* More Than a Piece of Paper
* The Payoff
* Where There's a Will
* Sharing is Caring

SIGNED, SEALED, DELIVERED

I think back to when I was studying for Level 1 and I was speaking with a client of mine who had just passed Level 3. Needless to say, I was impressed. I probably thought it wouldn't take me too long to join him basking in CFA glory. I remember saying, "What did you do when you found out you'd passed?" He said, "I was so goddamn relieved. I was like, just give me that charter and I am going to frame the sh*t out of that motherf**ker." That phrase stuck with me as I studied for the tests. I'm sure there are a thousand more eloquent ways to put it, but at the end of the day, I just wanted to "frame the sh*t out of that motherf**ker."

I've spoken with many charterholders over the years about what it was like to pass. As a candidate, you're understandably and endlessly curious about the subject. You're dedicating your life to this exam. You'd like to know that there is a pot of gold at the end of the rainbow, right?

One of my former colleagues, who was a classic overachiever and CFA charterholder, told me that she found out that she passed the CFA and got married in the same week. She truly wasn't sure which she was more excited about. Sounds crazy, and I'm sure she loves her husband, but when you've been through this process, such a statement oddly makes sense to you.

So how did I feel? Well, to some extent I'd say it was anti-climactic. At the beginning of August of that year, I left my job on Wall Street and relocated the family to Charlotte, North Carolina, where my wife wanted to move all along. Funny how that happens. We moved to be closer to my wife's family and because we thought it would be a much better lifestyle and a better place to raise a family. We busily began setting up a house and getting our son settled in.

In the midst of this major transition, I truthfully wasn't really thinking much about the CFA, though of course I had the results date circled on my calendar.

So that fateful day in mid-August, sitting in my new home in Charlotte, I received my email. I had a pretty good feeling about the test, but braced myself for disappointment.

This was *huge*. If it was a no-go, that was it. No more CFA dreams. No more long nights studying, weekends locked away with my books while my family went on without me. I sat down, took a deep breath, and opened it up. PASS. *Congratulations* and a blur of other positive words that could have said anything as far as I was concerned as long as they didn't say FAIL. I felt relief. I felt pride. I felt thankful. I had done it.

Finally. It was over.

I told my immediate family right away and everyone was so excited. I was grateful for their congratulations. I also reached out to a few other people to tell them the good news. One was the work colleague who'd failed Level 3 with me before. He passed too. I was so happy for him. It felt great to see someone pass who I knew had really worked hard for it.

I also reached out to two or three other former colleagues, and I almost felt guilty for hiding from them the fact that I had taken the exam. But they were happy for me and extended congratulations.

But that was it. I really wasn't looking for pats on the back. I didn't need to brag to the world on Facebook that I'd just passed this horrific test. I thought back on the quest for respect that I spoke of earlier; how I was dying for my buy-side clients and everyone else to think that I was smart. But the funny thing is, I no longer cared. I had zero desire to advertise the fact that I had passed the test. The only thing that was important to me was that *I* knew I had passed it. Me. This was my battle. It was me against my own demons. And I had conquered them.

Finding out you've passed the CFA is intense, no matter what else is going on in your life. Here's a helpful chart to translate what newly minted charterholders mean when they get their results.

What they say:	What they mean:
Oh, are the results out?	I just refreshed my email a hundred times.
Not even sure if I'll use it.	I already updated my LinkedIn profile.
It wasn't that hard.	I can't believe I passed.
I'm really lucky.	I worked my tail off and I deserve this.

BACK OF THE CLOSET

My charter showed up a few months later. It arrived in a cardboard tube in the mail on a very busy day. My wife and I were at home doing a million things and chasing our son around, and the cardboard tube sat for a few hours without being opened. Finally, I walked over to it and thought, "I just dedicated five years of my life to getting this piece of paper, and now I just let it sit around for a few hours without opening it?"

I opened the tube and here's what I saw:

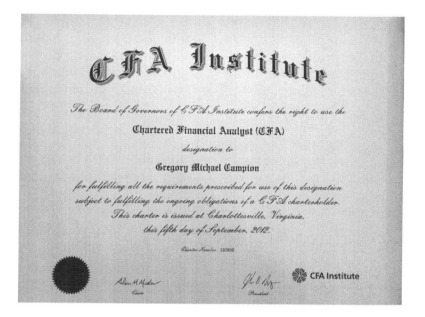

It was pretty cool to see my name in lights. I had imagined this day for years and here it was. I admired my accomplishment for all of a minute, then it went right back in the cardboard tube and subsequently took its illustrious place . . . in the back of my closet. That's right. I have yet to "frame the sh*t out of that motherf**ker." I suppose that if I find myself someday with a nice office with some spare wall space, well then, my charter may fill that space nicely. But then again, I've got a really cool picture of the first pitch of the 2004

World Series (the year the Red Sox broke "The Curse"), and I like staring at that just fine.

MORE THAN A PIECE OF PAPER

What I gained by taking the CFA exams was more than just a piece of paper. I obviously gained a ton of investment knowledge. Will I use it all? To be honest, probably not. There is a massive amount of detailed information contained in the curriculum. No single charterholder in existence has ever gone on to use *all* of it. Of course you never know more about it than the day you walk out the door from that exam. Naturally, you lose much of the knowledge, and that's to be expected. I have no idea what percentage of the curriculum I have retained. But the CFA process raises your level of understanding on a great many investment-related subjects, and you'll never lose *all* of that knowledge. If I was, say, a 6 on a scale of 10 in terms of investment knowledge when I started the process, maybe I am a 9 now that it's over, and I can't imagine falling below an 8 even if I gave up finance forever. Many of the most important concepts—valuing equities using the Gordon Growth Model or mastering how mortgage-backed securities exhibit negative convexity—well, those concepts are hammered so deeply into your head by the CFA exams that it's unlikely you'll forget them anytime soon, if ever.

Even if I were to walk away from finance forever, I feel like I can always look back to my CFA books and refresh my memory on the specifics of any one subject whenever I need to. It's funny, though. When I think of what I've gained, the actual investment knowledge is way down the list in terms of importance to me.

I've certainly gained the right to use "CFA" after my name. I passed the tests, I pay the dues, and I use it. I've got it on my CV, my email signature, and my LinkedIn profile. To some people who don't even know what the CFA is, I'm sure it's completely meaningless, but to those of us who have attempted to slay this beast, it means a great deal. Do I want people to look at my LinkedIn profile and say, "Hey, this guy's a CFA charterholder—he must be smart"? No, I'd like them to *know* that I am a hard worker. That's more important to me now.

Hi, my name is . . .

If you work your tail off to attain an MBA or CFA, then you'll want people to know about it. I'm not saying you should be ostentatious, but there's a certain amount of satisfaction that comes from getting the credit you deserve. Here are a few of my rules to help guide you in advertising your credentials:

- If you've earned your CFA charter or another professional designation, like the CAIA® or CIMA®, well then, use it! You should use it after your name in such places as email signatures, on your CV, and in your profile on sites like LinkedIn. You passed the test, you met the requirements, and you pay the dues. Get the credit you deserve!
- *Don't* use MBA after your name. Look, earning your MBA is a great achievement, but it's simply not convention to use it as part of one's name. When I see this, it has the opposite effect that I'm sure the person is trying to achieve. The exception for academic degrees is the PhD.
- *Don't* advertise on your CV or LinkedIn profile that you passed all three levels of the CFA on your first try. Quite frankly, it's a pretty darn impressive achievement. But just know that everyone who *did not* pass these exams on their first try will forever detest you. So as long as you're ok with that . . .

THE PAYOFF

The CFA is a door opener. If you're looking for a job, this is especially true. People are impressed with the credential without a doubt. Whether it's just getting over some recruiting hurdle where a company may be looking only for CFA charterholders, or mentioning it in an email to a senior person whose attention you are trying to get, it helps.

The CFA network is a great resource as well. First of all, having access to the CFA Institute's Jobline job board when you are looking for your next opportunity is huge. The employers on there are clearly seeking charterholders or those in pursuit of the designation. It's a great resource to check out to get a feel for the different types of employment opportunities available to charterholders and to see what types of companies are looking. I found it helpful in moving to a new location as it gave me another resource to explore potential opportunities.

The local CFA chapters are also pretty good. The local CFA society in North Carolina has proven to be a great networking resource. I've attended a few drinks events that they have put on, as well as their annual dinner. I've found it to be quite helpful in terms of meeting people and trying to get a better feel for what types of opportunities exist nearby. I would suggest joining your local chapter and getting involved with the networking events. You've got something in common with everyone there, so it's extremely easy to strike up a conversation with anyone. If you're speaking to a candidate, they'll probably want to hear about your experience. If you're speaking with another charterholder, you can discuss your battle scars. Inevitably, the conversation will move on to "What do you do?" and you'll end up expanding your network greatly.

So outside of the investment knowledge, the right to use the "CFA," and the ability to tap into local chapters and networks, there are also some really important intangible benefits, like respect, satisfaction, and confidence.

There's no question that earning the CFA charter wins you the respect of others. Ninety percent of the population probably doesn't know what the heck the CFA is, but the other ten percent think you're pretty darn impressive. I'm not saying that since I've attained my charter I've had hordes of groupies following me around asking me to sign their calculators, but I'm willing to bet that when people come across my LinkedIn profile, they are impressed to see that I've completed the program. Anything you can do to bolster your personal brand is a wise move, and for me, one major component was the CFA Program.

The other kind of respect that you gain is self-respect. I'm truly satisfied that I gave this test one more try. I'm proud of myself for sticking with it. I know I would have regretted quitting for the rest of my life. As I was pondering whether or not to take Level 3 that final time, I would cringe thinking about a future that would always have a footnote of failure. It gives me great pleasure now to think back on how I had the perseverance to give it one more try. I conquered my demons.

WHERE THERE'S A WILL

I won't sugarcoat the fact that you need to be incredibly self-disciplined to get your charter. When I signed up for that first CFA course, years before I ever sat for my Level 1 exam, I wasn't there yet. I felt overwhelmed by how difficult the process seemed. But by breaking the material down into achievable, manageable portions, I was able to build both my knowledge and endurance to succeed at the test.

I often hear people compare studying for these exams to the process of training for and running a marathon. I can imagine this is true. If you're not much of a runner, you need to start somewhere. Maybe you can barely run a mile or two, and the idea of running 26.2 miles just seems, well, impossible. But you make a plan. You set up a schedule. You organize your time and what you need to do to get to your goal, and then you stick with the plan. You make sacrifices to achieve your goals.

It's the same with the CFA. I was very disciplined with my planning. I'd stick to my schedule, and Lord knows I made sacrifices. I dealt with pain and disappointment and setbacks and failure. But I also learned perseverance and discipline. I learned how to pick myself up off the ground and figure out a way to keep going. These are very important skills to have in life. They make you stronger. When you inevitably encounter more pain and more disappointments and more setbacks in your life, you'll be prepared. You've been there before and you know what to do. Pick yourself up and keep going.

It sounds incredibly corny or cheesy or whatever you want to call it, but the CFA Program basically taught me that I can do *anything*. Well, maybe not anything. I'm PROBABLY not going to be a professional athlete. (But never say never.) I'm probably never going to be a Nobel Prize–winning mathematician either. But I *am* going to do many more amazing things in my time on this planet. I *am* going to conquer many more incredibly difficult tasks. Those tasks are going to seem nothing less than Herculean at first. When I tell people that I'm planning to undertake them, they'll be skeptical. They'll say, "Is that really a good idea?" But I'll know that I want to accomplish a goal. If I want to do it badly enough, I will.

Look, I'm not the world's smartest guy. Many people make their way through the CFA exams with much more ease than I was able to. This book was not really written for them. I admire the intellect of these folks, but I wrote this book for those of you who find the CFA process to be an epic struggle, one that tests your mettle and will to the very core. Those of you who have failed tests along the way, are struggling to decide whether or not to continue, and who have felt disappointment unlike you have ever experienced before. This book is for you. I have so much respect for you and I can truly feel your pain.

If you're still early in the process or haven't even signed up for the exams yet, the truth is that the CFA isn't for everyone. Think long and hard about whether or not you are on the right path. If you're not, re-route. Do you really want this? Are you really self-disciplined enough to achieve this goal? At the end of the day, is this the direction you really want your career to go in? You'll thank yourself later if you spend the time now thinking through these questions.

If you know you want the CFA with all your heart and that it will be a boon to both your career and your personal development, stick with it. Failure is terrible, but it's also an amazing teacher. I can tell you from personal experience that there is nothing more rewarding than putting everything you've got into something that you've failed at, and ultimately succeeding.

By picking yourself up off the ground and soldiering on, you'll learn much more about yourself than you can from any book.

My thoughts are with you. If you *really* want it, you can absolutely get through this. I wish you the best of luck!

SHARING IS CARING

If you have a CFA experience to share, I'd love to hear it. Has your CFA journey been similar to or completely different than mine? What did you give up? How did you have to sacrifice? Did you develop any foolproof strategies to help you master the material? You never know how your story or study tips might help someone else along.

Email me at: CFAConfidential@gmail.com

Chapter 8 Checklist:	
☑ **Do:**	☒ **Don't:**
☑ 1) Celebrate your achievement!	☒ 1) Be ostentatious.
☑ 2) Reflect on what you've really gained from the CFA Program.	☒ 2) Disregard some of the most important lessons.
☑ 3) Make use of the CFA network.	☒ 3) Be a hermit.
☑ 4) Be thankful to those who supported you.	☒ 4) Assume that you did this on your own.
☑ 5) Share your CFA story with me!	☒ 5) Keep it bottled up inside. It's just not healthy!

Acknowledgements

This book, like my CFA charter, would not have been possible without the help of others.

My wife, Whitney, has probably sacrificed as much if not more along the way than I have to make both of these dreams become reality. She also is awesome at making charts and graphs, which came in handy!

Additionally, I'd like to thank:

My son, Charlie, for being a good boy while daddy studied and wrote.

My parents and the rest of my family for all of their support.

My beta readers! These poor souls had the unenviable task of reading a very early version of *CFA Confidential*. Their suggestions and advice were incredibly valuable in helping to shape the final product. In many cases, they helped save me . . . from myself!

They are (in alphabetical order):

Naa-Sakle Akuete, Lisa Campion, Mary Campion, Ned Campion Jr., Ned Campion III, Whitney Campion, Brad Godfrey, Andy Rafal, Megan Taylor, Susan Taylor, William Taylor, and Elizabeth Wells.

Special thanks to:

My editor, Lindsey Alexander, for holding my hand during the process of writing my first book and for her incredibly valuable insights on everything from grammar to whether or not something was funny. (Usually, it was not.)

My book designer, Dedicated Book Services, for helping to bring this vision in my head into the real world.

And to you, the reader. This book was written for you. I hope it will help you in some small way.

Historical CFA Exam Pass Rates

Source: www.cfainstitute.org

CFA Candidates	ALL LEVELS		LEVEL I				LEVEL II				LEVEL III			
Year	Total	% Pass	Total	Pass	Fail	% Pass	Total	Pass	Fail	% Pass	Total	Pass	Fail	% Pass
1963	284	94%	—	—	—	0%	—	—	—	0%	284	268	16	94%
1964	1,732	84%	1,241	986	255	79%	302	283	19	94%	189	179	10	95%
1965	1,993	83%	767	649	118	85%	865	678	187	78%	361	329	32	91%
1966	2,010	75%	621	481	140	77%	708	469	239	66%	681	563	118	83%
1967	1,693	83%	594	423	171	71%	556	496	60	89%	543	491	52	90%
1968	1,579	73%	592	412	180	70%	447	334	113	75%	540	414	126	77%
1969	1,316	74%	556	409	147	74%	413	322	91	78%	347	237	110	68%
1970	1,409	67%	644	424	220	66%	372	285	87	77%	393	238	155	61%
1971	1,458	69%	755	464	291	61%	341	253	88	74%	362	288	74	80%
1972	1,486	70%	731	466	265	64%	461	354	107	77%	294	214	80	73%
1973	1,630	60%	721	432	289	60%	565	324	241	57%	344	222	122	65%
1974	1,797	74%	862	604	258	70%	511	377	134	74%	424	355	69	84%
1975	1,841	75%	808	568	240	70%	563	421	142	75%	470	393	77	84%
1976	1,706	76%	634	457	177	72%	641	477	164	74%	431	363	68	84%
1977	1,993	74%	667	421	246	63%	632	510	122	81%	694	540	154	78%
1978	2,008	73%	925	596	329	64%	444	379	65	85%	639	481	158	75%
1979	1,876	76%	824	522	302	63%	550	460	90	84%	502	441	61	88%
1980	1,985	73%	949	602	347	63%	528	407	121	77%	508	437	71	86%

CFA Candidates Year	ALL LEVELS		LEVEL I				LEVEL II				LEVEL III			
	Total	% Pass	Total	Pass	Fail	% Pass	Total	Pass	Fail	% Pass	Total	Pass	Fail	% Pass
1981	2,253	71%	1,107	677	430	61%	684	580	104	85%	462	340	122	74%
1982	2,886	64%	1,532	903	629	59%	714	489	225	68%	640	469	171	73%
1983	3,243	65%	1,655	1,082	573	65%	978	637	341	65%	610	392	218	64%
1984	4,030	63%	2,075	1,199	876	58%	1,147	701	446	61%	808	658	150	81%
1985	4,285	67%	2,186	1,317	869	60%	1,309	965	344	74%	790	579	211	73%
1986	4,837	65%	2,366	1,405	961	59%	1,379	884	495	64%	1,092	845	247	77%
1987	5,702	62%	3,095	1,782	1,313	58%	1,555	995	560	64%	1,052	755	297	72%
1988	7,091	59%	3,927	2,174	1,753	55%	1,946	1,163	783	60%	1,218	864	354	71%
1989	8,064	62%	4,149	2,237	1,912	54%	2,484	1,590	894	64%	1,431	1,133	298	79%
1990	8,760	64%	4,415	2,658	1,757	60%	2,522	1,594	928	63%	1,823	1,360	463	75%
1991	9,868	62%	4,950	3,087	1,863	62%	3,002	1,618	1,384	54%	1,916	1,436	480	75%
1992	10,518	65%	5,002	2,928	2,074	59%	3,503	2,258	1,245	64%	2,013	1,658	355	82%
1993	12,809	59%	6,588	3,616	2,972	55%	3,679	2,061	1,618	56%	2,542	1,936	606	76%
1994	15,413	52%	8,445	4,087	4,358	48%	4,418	2,109	2,309	48%	2,550	1,859	691	73%
1995	19,517	52%	11,341	5,750	5,591	51%	5,518	2,535	2,983	46%	2,658	1,860	798	70%
1996	24,600	58%	14,381	7,627	6,754	53%	7,098	4,596	2,502	65%	3,121	1,999	1,122	64%
1997	30,642	55%	16,833	8,847	7,986	53%	8,493	5,011	3,482	59%	5,316	3,119	2,197	59%
1998	38,689	60%	21,744	12,355	8,889	59%	10,295	6,433	3,862	62%	6,650	3,895	2,755	59%
1999	45,143	60%	23,199	14,757	8,442	64%	13,496	7,329	6,167	54%	8,448	5,015	3,433	59%
2000	53,345	55%	27,625	14,314	13,311	52%	16,036	8,636	7,400	54%	9,684	6,274	3,410	65%
2001	65,707	54%	36,317	17,726	18,591	49%	17,897	8,322	9,575	46%	11,493	9,410	2,083	82%

CFA Candidates	ALL LEVELS		LEVEL I				LEVEL II				LEVEL III			
Year	Total	% Pass	Total	Pass	Fail	% Pass	Total	Pass	Fail	% Pass	Total	Pass	Fail	% Pass
2002	76,231	47%	43,882	19,106	24,776	44%	22,163	10,418	11,745	47%	10,186	5,924	4,262	58%
2003A	67,279	49%	32,027	13,478	18,549	42%	22,232	10,432	11,800	47%	13,020	8,816	4,204	68%
2003B	20,657	40%	20,657	8,214	12,443	40%								
2004A	61,559	40%	24,211	8,262	15,949	34%	23,896	7,649	16,247	32%	13,452	8,669	4,783	64%
2004B	19,566	36%	19,566	7,128	12,438	36%								
2005A	58,908	48%	22,915	8,138	14,777	36%	24,891	13,938	10,953	56%	11,102	6,083	5,019	55%
2005B	21,127	34%	21,127	7,276	13,851	34%								
2006A	63,249	52%	26,467	10,602	15,865	40%	20,499	9,751	10,748	48%	16,283	12,314	3,969	76%
2006B	28,082	39%	28,082	10,905	17,177	39%								
2007A	71,897	42%	33,599	13,294	20,305	40%	25,521	10,156	15,365	40%	12,777	6,399	6,378	50%
2007B	37,573	39%	37,573	14,831	22,742	39%								
2008A	92,081	42%	44,063	15,311	28,752	35%	33,449	15,243	18,206	46%	14,569	7,720	6,849	53%
2008B	49,797	35%	49,797	17,612	32,185	35%								
2009A	104,116	45%	45,682	21,034	24,648	46%	38,998	15,892	23,106	41%	19,436	9,597	9,839	49%
2009B	44,209	34%	44,209	14,884	29,325	34%								
2010A	111,731	42%	46,863	19,656	27,207	42%	43,406	16,995	26,411	39%	21,462	9,881	11,581	46%
2010B	46,785	36%	46,785	17,009	29,776	36%								
2011A	115,027	43%	48,068	18,881	29,187	39%	44,175	19,009	25,166	43%	22,784	11,567	11,217	51%
2011B	49,380	38%	49,380	18,736	30,644	38%								

CFA Candidates	ALL LEVELS			LEVEL I				LEVEL II				LEVEL III			
Year	Total	% Pass	Total	Pass	Fail	% Pass	Total	Pass	Fail	% Pass	Total	Pass	Fail	% Pass
2012A	119,446	43%	49,445	18,968	30,477	38%	45,247	19,194	26,053	42%	24,754	12,870	11,884	52%
2012B	48,981	37%	48,981	18,106	30,875	37%								
1963-2012B	1,714,879	46%	999,202	421,375	577,827	42%	461,529	216,012	245,517	47%	254,148	152,149	101,999	60%
2003-2012B*	1,231,450	42%	739,497	282,325	457,172	38%	322,314	138,259	184,055	43%	169,639	93,916	75,723	55%

NOTES

NOTES

NOTES

Made in the USA
Lexington, KY
19 July 2014